COPENHAGEN

TRAVEL GUIDE

2024/2025

A Guide to the City's Hidden Gems, Cultural Treasures, Outdoor Activities, Culinary Delights, Nature and Sustainable Travel Tips

DIANE W. CLARK

Copyright © 2024 by Diane W. Clark

All rights reserved. No part of this book may be reproduced, distributed, or transmitted in any form or by any means, including photocopying, recording, or other electronic or mechanical methods, without the prior written permission of the publisher, except in the case of brief quotations embodied in critical reviews and specific other noncommercial uses permitted by copyright law

TABLE OF CONTENTS

INTRODUCTION 7
    The Essence of Copenhagen: A Brief Overview 10
    Why Visit Copenhagen: Highlights of the City 12
    How to Use This Guide: Tips for Navigating the City 15

CHAPTER 1 18
PLANNING YOUR TRIP 18
    Best time to visit Copenhagen 18
    Duration of your trip 23
    Copenhagen on a budget 26
    Choosing the right tour package 29
    Entry and visa requirements 32

CHAPTER 2 35
GETTING TO COPENHAGEN 35
    Arriving by Air: Copenhagen Airport (CPH) 35
    Choosing The Best Flight 37
    Copenhagen airport: Arrival and Orientation 41
    Journey To Copenhagen 43
    Arriving by Train: International and Domestic Connections. 45
    Arriving by Bus 47
    Arriving by Sea: Ferry and Cruise Options 49
    Getting Around: Public Transportation, Cycling, and Walking 51

CHAPTER 3 53
ACCOMMODATION OPTION 53
CHAPTER 4 61
NEIGHBORHOOD OF COPENHAGEN 61
    Indre By: The Historic Heart of Copenhagen 61

Vesterbro: The Trendy and Bohemian District.................. 64
Nørrebro: Multicultural and Vibrant.................................. 66
Østerbro: Chic and Family-Friendly.................................. 69
Christianshavn: Canals and Counterculture................... 71
Frederiksberg: Green Spaces and Regal Charm............ 73
Amager: The Emerging Area with a Beachside Vibe....... 75

CHAPTER 5..77

TOP ATTRACTION..77

The Little Mermaid: Copenhagen's Iconic Symbol........... 77
Tivoli Gardens: The World's Second-Oldest Amusement Park.. 79
Nyhavn: The Colorful Waterfront and its History.............. 82
Rosenborg Castle: A Glimpse into Royal Life.................. 85
Amalienborg Palace: The Royal Family's Winter Residence... 88
The Round Tower: A Panoramic View of the City............ 90
Christiansborg Palace: The Seat of Danish Parliament... 93

CHAPTER 6..96

MUSEUMS AND ART GALLERIES..96

The National Museum of Denmark.................................. 96
The Danish National Gallery (SMK)................................. 99
The Ny Carlsberg Glyptotek... 101
The Louisiana Museum of Modern Art........................... 103
Designmuseum Danmark... 106
The David Collection.. 108

CHAPTER 7.. 111

CULINARY SCENE... 111

Traditional Danish Cuisine: Smørrebrød, Frikadeller, and More...111

Copenhagen's Michelin-Starred Restaurants................114
Street Food: The Best Markets and Food Halls.............118
Cafés and Bakeries: Hygge and Danish Pastries..........120
The Craft Beer Scene: Breweries and Beer Bars..........122
Festivals and Traditions:..124

CHAPTER 8..126
DAY TRIPS FROM COPENHAGEN..................................126
Kronborg Castle: The Home of Hamlet.........................126
Malmö, Sweden: A Quick Trip Across the Øresund Bridge.. 130
Dragør: A Charming Village Near the Sea......................132
The Louisiana Museum of Modern Art: Art and Nature..134

CHAPTER 9..136
OUTDOOR ACTIVITIES..136
Copenhagen's Parks and Gardens................................136
Cycling in Copenhagen: Routes and Bike Rentals........138
Canal Tours: Discovering the City from the Water.........140
The Beaches: Amager Strandpark and Beyond.............142
Exploring Copenhagen's Islands: Refshaleøen and Paper Island..144

CHAPTER 10..146
COPENHAGEN FOR DIFFERENT TRAVELERS...............146
Copenhagen with Kids: Family-Friendly Activities.........146
Romantic Copenhagen: Couples' Getaway...................148
Copenhagen for Solo Travelers: Safe and Fun.............150

CHAPTER 11..153
SUSTAINABLE TRAVEL IN COPENHAGEN.....................153
Eco-Friendly Accommodation......................................153
Green Transportation: Biking, Walking, and Public Transit..

156
    Responsible Tourism: Minimizing Your Footprint........... 159
CHAPTER 12..162
PRACTICAL INFORMATION... 162
    Currency and Budgeting: Navigating Danish Kroner..... 162
    Language: Key Danish Phrases and English Proficiency.... 165
    Safety and Health: Staying Safe in Copenhagen........... 167
    Etiquette and Local Customs.. 169
    Useful Apps And Website..171
CONCLUSION...174
    MAP.. 178

INTRODUCTION

Copenhagen is a city that effortlessly blends the old with the new, where history and modernity coexist in perfect harmony. The city's charm lies in its cobblestone streets, colorful buildings, and the gentle rhythm of life along its canals. As you walk through its neighborhoods, you'll notice the mix of medieval architecture and contemporary design, each corner revealing something unique and captivating. It's a place where you can feel the pulse of a vibrant urban culture while also sensing the echoes of its rich past.

I'd always been a fan of fantasy stories, especially Game of Thrones, with its tales of the North. So, when I was thinking about my next travel destination, Copenhagen seemed like the perfect choice—a city in the north, full of history and mystery.

But what I found when I arrived was even more magical than I expected.

As the plane began to descend, I looked out the window and saw the city spread out like something from a fairy tale. Church spires pointed up to the sky, and the streets below looked like they had stories to tell. When I stepped out of the airport, a cool breeze greeted me, carrying the fresh scent of pine and the nearby sea. It was like stepping into another world.

On my first day, I wandered through Nyhavn, the picturesque canal district with its rows of colorful houses. As I walked, I imagined dragons flying overhead and knights on the cobblestone streets. Of course, there were no dragons, but the magic of the place was undeniable.

Over the next few days, I explored more of Copenhagen. I delved into Viking history at the National Museum of Denmark, marveled at the enchanting Tivoli Gardens, and visited the iconic Little Mermaid statue, which seemed to capture the spirit of the city. But what really stood out were the people—their warmth, friendliness, and the way they embraced life's simple pleasures.

As I sat in a cozy café, sipping hot chocolate, I realized that Copenhagen had exceeded all my expectations. It was a city that felt timeless, where past and present merged beautifully. It's a hidden gem in the Nordic winter, full of wonder and adventure.

In this guide, I want to share my experiences and insights with you, to help you discover the magic of Copenhagen for yourself. You'll find tips on where to go, what to see, and how to truly immerse yourself in the city's unique charm. So, get ready to embark on your own adventure in this enchanting city. Let Copenhagen capture your heart, just as it did mine, and keep reading to uncover all the wonders this city has to offer.

The Essence of Copenhagen: A Brief Overview

Copenhagen is a city that captures the essence of Scandinavian beauty and culture. Imagine a place where the streets are lined with charming, colorful buildings, and the air is filled with the crisp freshness of the sea. This is a city where history and modern life blend seamlessly, creating an atmosphere that is both relaxed and vibrant.

The heart of Copenhagen lies in its people and their way of life. The Danes have a word, "hygge," which describes a feeling of coziness and contentment. You can see this everywhere in the city, from the warm glow of candles in windows to the inviting atmosphere of cafes where locals gather to enjoy a cup of coffee and good conversation. This sense of comfort and community is what makes Copenhagen so special.

As you explore the city, you'll notice how easy it is to get around. Copenhagen is known for being bike-friendly, and many people choose to cycle through its streets. The public transportation system is also efficient, making it simple to move from one part of the city to another. Whether you're riding a bike along the harbor or taking a leisurely stroll through one of the city's many parks, you'll feel a connection to the rhythm of life in Copenhagen.

One of the city's most iconic sights is Nyhavn, a historic waterfront district that is as picturesque as it gets. The colorful townhouses that line the canal are a favorite subject for photographers, and the area is filled with restaurants where you can enjoy a meal while watching the boats go by. It's the perfect place to soak in the beauty of the city and get a taste of its maritime history.

Copenhagen is also a city of contrasts. While it is steeped in history, with centuries-old castles and cobblestone streets, it is also a hub of modern design and innovation. The architecture here is a mix of old and new, from the grand palaces to cutting-edge buildings like the Danish Opera House. This blend of tradition and modernity gives the city a unique character that is both timeless and forward-thinking.

For those interested in culture, Copenhagen offers a wealth of museums, galleries, and theaters. The National Museum of Denmark takes you on a journey through the country's history, while the Louisiana Museum of Modern Art showcases contemporary works in a stunning seaside setting. The city's vibrant arts scene is complemented by its culinary offerings, with everything from Michelin-starred restaurants to cozy bakeries serving up traditional Danish pastries.

But what truly sets Copenhagen apart is the atmosphere. There is a sense of calm and order here, a respect for nature and the environment that is evident in the clean streets and the city's many green spaces. Yet, at the same time, there is a spirit of creativity and innovation that makes the city feel alive with possibilities.

Whether you're interested in history, culture, or simply experiencing the Scandinavian way of life, Copenhagen offers something for everyone. It's a city where you can explore at your own pace, discover hidden gems around every corner, and leave with a sense of having experienced something truly special. If you're looking for a destination that combines beauty, culture, and a sense of well-being, Copenhagen is a place you won't want to miss.

Why Visit Copenhagen: Highlights of the City

Copenhagen is a city that effortlessly blends old-world charm with modern innovation, making it a must-visit destination for any traveler. The city is known for its rich history, stunning architecture, vibrant culture, and a strong commitment to sustainability. Whether you're drawn to its historic sites, love exploring unique neighborhoods, or simply want to experience the famous Danish concept of "hygge," Copenhagen offers something for everyone. Here's why you should visit this captivating city and what highlights you can't miss.

One of the first things you'll notice about Copenhagen is its unique mix of historic and contemporary architecture. Walking through the city, you'll encounter grand palaces and churches that stand alongside sleek, modern buildings. The Amalienborg Palace, home to the Danish royal family, is a perfect example of this blend. Located at Amalienborg Slotsplads, 1257 København K, it's a beautiful sight, especially during the Changing of the Guard ceremony at noon. Nearby, you can marvel at the striking modern design of the Copenhagen Opera House, located at Ekvipagemester Vej 10, 1438 København K, which offers stunning views across the harbor.

The city's most iconic landmark is the Little Mermaid statue, located at Langelinie, 2100 København Ø. Inspired by Hans Christian Andersen's famous fairy tale, this statue is a symbol of Copenhagen and a popular spot for photos. While it may be smaller than you expect, its significance and the beautiful waterfront setting make it a must-see.

Copenhagen is also home to a vibrant cultural scene, with numerous museums and galleries to explore. The National Museum of Denmark at Ny Vestergade 10, 1471 København K, is a great place to start if you're interested in the country's history and culture. From Viking artifacts to exhibitions on modern Danish life, the museum offers a comprehensive overview of Denmark's past and present. For art lovers, the Ny Carlsberg Glyptotek at Dantes Plads 7, 1556 København V, is a treasure trove of classical sculptures and French Impressionist paintings.

Another highlight of Copenhagen is its lively neighborhoods, each with its own distinct character. Nyhavn is perhaps the most famous, with its colorful townhouses and bustling harbor. This area is perfect for a leisurely stroll, enjoying a meal at one of the many outdoor cafes, or taking a boat tour to see the city from the water. For a more alternative vibe, head to the district of Vesterbro. Once a red-light district, Vesterbro has transformed into one of Copenhagen's coolest areas, filled with trendy cafes, vintage shops, and vibrant nightlife. The Meatpacking District, known locally as Kødbyen, is particularly popular for its eclectic mix of restaurants and bars.

If you're looking for a peaceful escape from the city's hustle and bustle, the Tivoli Gardens is a must-visit. Located at Vesterbrogade 3, 1630 København V, this historic amusement park is one of the oldest in the world and has a charm that appeals to visitors of all ages. Whether you're there to enjoy the thrilling rides, watch a live performance, or simply relax in the beautifully landscaped gardens, Tivoli is a place where the magic of Copenhagen truly comes alive.

Copenhagen is also a paradise for food enthusiasts. The city is renowned for its culinary scene, which ranges from Michelin-starred restaurants to cozy cafes serving traditional Danish pastries. Don't miss the chance to try smørrebrød, the classic open-faced sandwich, at one of the city's many lunch spots. For a more immersive experience, visit Torvehallerne at Frederiksborggade 21, 1362 København K, a bustling food market where you can sample everything from fresh seafood to artisanal chocolates.

What truly sets Copenhagen apart, though, is its commitment to sustainability and the high quality of life enjoyed by its residents. The city is consistently ranked as one of the happiest in the world, and it's easy to see why. Biking is a way of life here, with dedicated lanes and bike rentals available throughout the city. Green spaces are abundant, and the harbor is so clean that you can swim in it during the warmer months. This dedication to the environment and well-being is something that visitors often find inspiring and refreshing.

In Copenhagen, you'll find a city that invites you to slow down and savor the moment. Whether you're exploring its historic landmarks, indulging in its culinary delights, or simply soaking in the relaxed atmosphere, Copenhagen offers a unique and memorable experience. It's a city that combines the best of both worlds—rich history and forward-thinking innovation—making it a destination you'll want to return to again and again.

How to Use This Guide: Tips for Navigating the City

To make the most of your time in Copenhagen, this guide will be your companion, offering you all the essential information you need to navigate the city with ease. Whether you're here for a few days or planning an extended stay, these tips will help you enjoy every moment.

First, let's talk about getting around. Copenhagen is known for being a bike-friendly city, and cycling is one of the best ways to explore. You can rent a bike from many shops around the city, or use one of the popular bike-sharing services like Donkey Republic. Biking in Copenhagen is safe and easy, with dedicated bike lanes on most streets. If you're not a fan of cycling, the public transportation system is excellent. The metro, buses, and trains are all well-connected, clean, and efficient. You can purchase a Copenhagen Card, which gives you unlimited access to public transport as well as free entry to many attractions. The metro runs 24 hours a day, so it's convenient no matter when you need to travel.

When planning your itinerary, remember that Copenhagen is a compact city. Most of the major attractions are within walking distance of each other, so you won't need to spend a lot of time in transit. This makes it easy to explore different neighborhoods in a single day. For example, you can start your morning in the historic center around Kongens Nytorv, wander through the picturesque streets of Nyhavn, and then head over to Christianshavn for a leisurely afternoon stroll along the canals.

If you're interested in visiting museums, palaces, or other popular attractions, it's a good idea to check their opening hours in advance. Many places are closed on Mondays, and some have shorter hours during the winter months. Buying tickets online can also save you time, especially for popular sites like Tivoli Gardens or the Rosenborg Castle. And speaking of tickets, don't forget to take advantage of combo deals or passes that offer entry to multiple attractions at a discounted rate.

As you explore Copenhagen, you'll quickly notice that the Danes value their environment. Recycling, using reusable bags, and minimizing waste are all part of daily life here. It's easy to join in and make your visit more eco-friendly. Carry a refillable water bottle, as tap water in Copenhagen is clean and safe to drink. Many cafes also offer discounts if you bring your own cup, so it's worth packing one if you enjoy coffee on the go.

One of the best ways to experience Copenhagen is by blending in with the locals. Danish culture is known for its concept of "hygge," which roughly translates to a feeling of coziness and contentment. You'll find hygge in the warm atmosphere of cafes, in the candlelit dinners, and in the simple pleasure of enjoying the city's parks and public spaces. Take time to slow down, relax, and soak in the peaceful vibe that makes Copenhagen so special.

Finally, don't be afraid to get off the beaten path. While the guide will lead you to the city's most famous landmarks, Copenhagen has plenty of hidden gems waiting to be discovered. Whether it's a small gallery tucked away in a quiet street, a local bakery with the best pastries you've ever tasted, or a peaceful spot by the water where you can watch the sunset, these little surprises are often the most memorable parts of a trip.

Using this guide, you'll have everything you need to navigate Copenhagen confidently and comfortably. The city is welcoming, easy to explore, and full of experiences that will leave a lasting impression. So, grab your map, hop on a bike, or take a leisurely walk, and let Copenhagen reveal itself to you, one delightful moment at a time.

CHAPTER 1.
PLANNING YOUR TRIP

Best time to visit Copenhagen

Copenhagen is a city that offers something special in every season, making it an enchanting destination year-round. Each season brings its own unique charm, atmosphere, and experiences, giving travelers different reasons to fall in love with the Danish capital. Whether you're looking for vibrant street life, cozy winter traditions, or picturesque landscapes, understanding the best times to visit Copenhagen can help you tailor your trip to match your interests and preferences.

Spring in Copenhagen feels like a breath of fresh air after the long winter months. The city awakens with a burst of color as parks and gardens bloom with tulips, daffodils, and cherry blossoms. The weather in spring is mild, with temperatures gradually rising from around 5°C (41°F) in March to 15°C (59°F) by May. Days become longer, and the city's outdoor spaces fill with locals and visitors eager to soak up the sunshine.

In spring, layers are your best friend. Bring a light jacket or sweater for cooler mornings and evenings, along with comfortable shoes for exploring the city on foot. An umbrella or rain jacket is also a good idea, as spring showers are common.

Spring is a wonderful time to explore Copenhagen's gardens and parks. The King's Garden (Kongens Have) and the

Botanical Garden are particularly beautiful during this season. If you're visiting in April, don't miss the cherry blossoms at Bispebjerg Cemetery, a local favorite for a springtime stroll. The city also hosts various events, such as the CPH:DOX documentary film festival in March and the Distortion festival in late May, which transforms the streets into a lively celebration of music and culture.

Spring is a shoulder season in Copenhagen, meaning the crowds are moderate, and prices are reasonable. You'll find more availability in hotels and shorter lines at popular attractions compared to the peak summer months. This makes spring an excellent choice for travelers who want to experience the city's vibrant atmosphere without the summer rush.

Compared to summer, spring in Copenhagen is quieter and more relaxed. It's an ideal time to visit if you prefer a laid-back atmosphere with the opportunity to see the city's natural beauty in bloom. However, if you're looking for warmer weather and more outdoor events, summer might be a better fit for you.

Summer in Copenhagen is nothing short of magical. The city comes alive with endless daylight, thanks to the long Scandinavian summer days where the sun sets as late as 10 PM. Temperatures are comfortably warm, averaging between 17°C (63°F) and 22°C (72°F), making it the perfect season for outdoor activities and festivals.

Pack light, breathable clothing for the warm days, but bring a light jacket or sweater for the cooler evenings. Sunglasses, sunscreen, and comfortable walking shoes are must-haves, as you'll likely spend a lot of time outdoors.

Summer is festival season in Copenhagen. The city buzzes with energy during events like the Copenhagen Jazz Festival in July, which brings world-class musicians to venues all over the city. Tivoli Gardens also hosts summer concerts and fireworks displays, making it a must-visit during this season. Don't miss the chance to relax like a local by picnicking in one of the city's many parks or taking a swim in the clean, refreshing harbor.

Summer is the peak tourist season in Copenhagen, so expect larger crowds and higher prices, especially in popular areas like Nyhavn and Tivoli Gardens. To avoid the busiest times, consider visiting attractions early in the morning or later in the afternoon. Booking accommodations and event tickets well in advance is advisable during this season.

If you love warm weather, long days, and a lively atmosphere, summer is the best time to visit Copenhagen. However, if you prefer fewer crowds and more budget-friendly options, spring or autumn might be more suitable for your travel style.

Autumn in Copenhagen is a season of change, as the city's parks and streets are transformed by a palette of red, orange, and yellow. The air becomes crisp, and the days start to shorten, creating a cozy atmosphere that's perfect for exploring the city's cultural attractions and indulging in the Danish tradition of hygge. Temperatures range from 10°C (50°F) in September to 5°C (41°F) in November, with occasional rain showers adding to the autumnal mood.

Layering is key in autumn. Bring a warm jacket, scarves, and comfortable shoes for walking on potentially wet streets. An umbrella is also handy, as autumn can be rainy.

Autumn is a great time to explore Copenhagen's museums and indoor attractions. The National Gallery of Denmark (SMK) and the Ny Carlsberg Glyptotek offer excellent escapes from the cooler weather. October is particularly festive, with Halloween celebrations at Tivoli Gardens, where the park is transformed into a spooky wonderland. November marks the beginning of the Christmas season, with holiday markets popping up around the city, including the popular one at Højbro Plads.

Autumn is a quieter time in Copenhagen, with fewer tourists than in summer. This means lower prices for accommodations and less crowded attractions, making it an ideal time for budget-conscious travelers or those who prefer a more tranquil visit.

Autumn offers a balance between the lively summer season and the quiet winter months. It's a wonderful time to visit if you enjoy cultural experiences, scenic walks through colorful parks, and the cozy atmosphere that defines Danish life during this time of year.

Winter in Copenhagen is a time of warmth and coziness, despite the cold weather. The city embraces the season with festive lights, Christmas markets, and the spirit of hygge. Temperatures typically range from 0°C (32°F) to 5°C (41°F), and while snow is not guaranteed, it adds a magical touch to the city when it falls.

Pack warm clothing, including a heavy coat, gloves, hats, and scarves. Thermal layers and waterproof boots are also recommended to keep you comfortable as you explore the city in chilly weather.

Winter in Copenhagen is all about embracing the season's traditions. The city's Christmas markets, such as the one at Nyhavn and Tivoli Gardens, are a must-visit for their festive atmosphere, handcrafted goods, and delicious treats like æbleskiver (Danish pancake balls) and gløgg (mulled wine). After Christmas, the city quiets down, making it a perfect time to explore museums, cozy cafes, and indoor attractions. January and February are great months to enjoy winter sales, with discounts at many of the city's shops.

Winter is the off-season in Copenhagen, meaning fewer tourists and lower prices. This makes it an excellent time to visit if you're looking for a more intimate experience of the city and are willing to brave the cold.

Winter offers a completely different experience from the other seasons, with a focus on indoor activities, festive traditions, and the Danish art of hygge. If you're drawn to cozy winter vibes and don't mind the cold, this season will provide you with a unique and memorable visit.

Each season in Copenhagen offers something different, catering to various preferences and travel styles. Whether you're drawn to the lively summer festivals, the blooming beauty of spring, the colorful tranquility of autumn, or the cozy charm of winter, Copenhagen has a season that will make your visit unforgettable. Understanding these seasonal highlights will help you choose the best time to experience all that this beautiful city has to offer.

Duration of your trip

When planning a trip to Copenhagen, the duration of your stay can significantly impact how much of the city you can experience. Copenhagen is a city rich in history, culture, and charm, and how long you decide to stay will determine how deeply you can immerse yourself in its offerings. Whether you have just a weekend or an entire week, there's a perfect itinerary to suit your travel goals.

For those with just a weekend to spare, Copenhagen is compact enough to give you a taste of its most famous sights and experiences. In two or three days, you can explore iconic attractions like Nyhavn, the colorful harbor that's perhaps the city's most photographed spot, and Tivoli Gardens, the world's second-oldest amusement park. A visit to the Little Mermaid statue, inspired by Hans Christian Andersen's fairy tale, is also a must. You can easily spend a morning wandering through the historic streets of the city center, perhaps visiting the Royal Palace of Amalienborg or the Rundetårn (Round Tower) for panoramic views of the city.

In the evenings, dining at one of Copenhagen's many Michelin-starred restaurants or enjoying a canal cruise under the city's twinkling lights can round out your short visit perfectly. While a weekend will only scratch the surface, it's enough to capture the essence of Copenhagen's charm and leave you wanting more.

If you have four to five days in Copenhagen, you can explore the city more leisurely and delve into some of its more unique neighborhoods and lesser-known attractions. With this time, you can venture beyond the central sights and spend a day in the hipster district of Vesterbro, known for its trendy cafes, street art, and the Meatpacking District, which has been transformed into a hub for nightlife and dining. A visit to the Carlsberg Brewery for a tour and tasting session is a fun way to spend an afternoon.

You could also dedicate a day to the artistic and free-spirited community of Christiania, a fascinating area known for its alternative lifestyle and colorful murals. Another half-day could be spent exploring the National Museum of Denmark or the Danish Design Museum, where you can gain insights into the country's rich history and contributions to global design.

With a longer stay of six to seven days or more, you can truly immerse yourself in the Copenhagen experience. This duration allows you to take day trips to nearby destinations like the stunning Louisiana Museum of Modern Art, located on the coast just 35 kilometers north of the city, or the historic Kronborg Castle in Helsingør, famously known as the setting of Shakespeare's Hamlet. You could also visit the quaint town of Roskilde, just a short train ride away, where you can explore the Viking Ship Museum and the impressive Roskilde Cathedral, a UNESCO World Heritage site.

During a week-long stay, you'll have ample time to explore Copenhagen's many parks and gardens, such as the peaceful Frederiksberg Gardens or the sprawling green spaces of Fælledparken. You can also take in more of the city's culinary scene, perhaps indulging in a food tour to sample Danish specialties like smørrebrød (open-faced sandwiches) and Danish pastries. There's also time to enjoy leisurely bike rides through the city, which is famously bike-friendly, and to relax by the water at Islands Brygge, a popular spot for locals in the summer.

In addition to these activities, a longer visit allows for spontaneous discoveries—those hidden cafes, local shops, and quiet corners of the city that make your trip truly personal and memorable. Whether you're sipping coffee at a quiet cafe or joining locals for a swim in the harbor, you'll have the luxury of time to experience Copenhagen like a local.

Ultimately, the duration of your trip to Copenhagen will depend on your interests and how much of the city you want to explore. Whether you have a brief visit or an extended stay, Copenhagen has the flexibility to offer an enriching experience at any pace. With a short visit, you'll capture the highlights; with more time, you'll uncover the city's deeper layers and its true essence.

Copenhagen on a budget

Exploring Copenhagen on a budget is not only possible but can also be incredibly rewarding. With its rich history, vibrant culture, and picturesque landscapes, the city offers numerous opportunities to experience its charm without breaking the bank. Here's how you can make the most of your visit while keeping your costs low.

Timing your visit to Copenhagen is one of the most effective ways to save money. The shoulder seasons, particularly spring (April to May) and autumn (September to October), are ideal for budget-conscious travelers. During these times, the weather is mild, the city is less crowded, and accommodation prices are generally lower than in the peak summer months. Spring brings blooming flowers and longer daylight hours, perfect for outdoor activities, while autumn offers crisp air and colorful foliage. Both seasons provide a more relaxed atmosphere, allowing you to explore without the rush of summer tourists. Additionally, some attractions and accommodations offer lower rates during these periods, making it easier to stretch your budget.

When it comes to finding affordable accommodation in Copenhagen, there are several options to consider. Hostels are a popular choice for budget travelers, offering both dormitory-style and private rooms at reasonable prices. For example, the Copenhagen Downtown Hostel, located in the heart of the city, offers dorm beds starting around DKK 150 (approximately 20 euros) per night, with private rooms available for a bit more. Guesthouses and vacation rentals are also good alternatives. Websites like Airbnb offer a range of budget-friendly apartments and rooms, often with the added benefit of kitchen facilities, allowing you to save on meals by cooking your own. Another option is to stay in the city's outlying neighborhoods, where prices are typically lower than in the city center. Areas like Nørrebro or Amager provide more affordable lodging while still being well-connected to the main attractions by public transport.

When planning activities in Copenhagen, there are plenty of ways to enjoy the city's highlights without spending a fortune. Many of Copenhagen's most iconic attractions are free to visit. For instance, you can take a leisurely stroll through the colorful Nyhavn harbor, visit the Little Mermaid statue, or explore the historic grounds of the Christiansborg Palace. The city is also home to numerous parks and green spaces, such as the King's Garden (Kongens Have) and Frederiksberg Gardens, where you can relax and soak in the local atmosphere at no cost. Copenhagen is known for its bike-friendly culture, and renting a bike for a day is an affordable way to explore the city's neighborhoods. You can also take advantage of free walking tours that depart daily from various locations, offering insights into the city's history and culture from knowledgeable guides. If you're interested in museums, consider visiting on a Wednesday, when several museums, including the National Museum of Denmark and the Ny Carlsberg Glyptotek, offer free admission.

Dining on a budget in Copenhagen doesn't mean compromising on quality. The city has a vibrant food scene with plenty of options that cater to budget-conscious travelers. Street food markets like Reffen, located on the Refshaleøen island, offer a variety of international cuisines at affordable prices, with meals typically costing around DKK 75-100 (10-13 euros). Smørrebrød, traditional Danish open-faced sandwiches, are another budget-friendly option, often available at cafes and small eateries for under DKK 50 (around 7 euros) each. For a more immersive experience, visit local supermarkets or bakeries to pick up ingredients for a picnic. Grab some fresh bread, cheese, and pastries, and enjoy your meal in one of Copenhagen's many parks. This is a great way to experience the local flavors while keeping costs down. Another tip is to dine at lunch rather than dinner, as many restaurants offer lunch specials at a fraction of the dinner prices.

Getting around Copenhagen on a budget is straightforward, thanks to the city's efficient public transport system and bike-friendly infrastructure. The Copenhagen Card is an excellent investment for those planning to visit multiple attractions, as it provides free entry to more than 80 attractions and unlimited travel on public transport. Prices for the card start at DKK 399 (around 54 euros) for 24 hours, but the savings can quickly add up if you plan to visit several sites. Alternatively, renting a bike is a cost-effective way to explore the city, with daily rentals starting around DKK 80 (11 euros). Copenhagen is compact and walkable, so many attractions are easily accessible on foot, further reducing transportation costs.

In summary, exploring Copenhagen on a budget is all about smart planning and making the most of the city's many free or low-cost attractions. By timing your visit during the shoulder seasons, choosing budget-friendly accommodation, seeking out affordable dining options, and taking advantage of cost-effective transportation, you can experience the best of Copenhagen without overspending. This vibrant city offers a wealth of experiences that don't require a lavish budget, proving that with a little planning, a memorable and enriching visit is well within reach.

Choosing the right tour package

Selecting the best tour packages for Copenhagen can transform your trip into a memorable adventure. Here's a detailed guide to help you navigate the options and find the perfect tour for your visit.

Copenhagen offers a range of tour packages to suit various interests and preferences. Guided tours are among the most popular choices. These tours typically include a knowledgeable guide who provides insights and stories about the city's history, culture, and landmarks. Guided tours can be a great way to cover major attractions like the Tivoli Gardens, the Little Mermaid statue, and Nyhavn. They usually last from a few hours to a full day and can range in cost from $50 to $150 per person, depending on the length and inclusivity of the tour.

Self-guided walking tours are another option, allowing you to explore the city at your own pace. These tours often come with a detailed map or audio guide that helps you navigate and learn about key sights without a fixed schedule. They are ideal for independent travelers who prefer flexibility. Costs for self-guided tours can be lower, often between $20 and $50, and you might only need to pay for entry fees to specific attractions.

Adventure excursions cater to those looking for unique and active experiences. These can include bike tours through the city, boat tours along the canals, or even day trips to nearby attractions like the Louisiana Museum of Modern Art. Adventure tours can vary significantly in price and duration, from a few hours to a whole day, with prices ranging from $60 to $200. These tours often include equipment rental and sometimes refreshments.

When choosing a tour package, consider your travel style and group composition. Families with children might prefer tours that offer a mix of educational and fun activities, like visits to the National Museum or Tivoli Gardens, which can be enjoyable for all ages. Couples might enjoy romantic boat tours through the canals or guided food tours exploring local culinary delights. Solo adventurers might find self-guided tours or small group excursions ideal for meeting new people and exploring at their own pace. Groups traveling together may benefit from private tours that can be customized to their interests and schedule.

Seasonal variations also play a role in selecting the right tour package. During the spring and summer, Copenhagen is lively with outdoor festivals and extended daylight hours, making it perfect for bike and boat tours. In contrast, autumn offers a more relaxed pace with fewer tourists, and winter brings a magical atmosphere with Christmas markets and festive lights. Some tours might be seasonal, such as boat tours that operate mainly in warmer months, while others, like museum visits, are available year-round.

Local insights can greatly enhance your experience. Local guides often have the best tips on hidden gems and lesser-known tours that might not be widely advertised. For example, a canal tour that explores lesser-known waterways can offer a unique perspective of the city. Previous travelers' reviews can also provide valuable information on tour quality and what to expect, helping you make an informed decision.

When booking a tour package, look for reputable tour operators with positive reviews and clear details about what's included. Booking in advance can often secure better rates and ensure availability, especially during peak travel seasons. Websites that specialize in tours or local travel agencies can be good resources. Be sure to check cancellation policies and any additional costs that may arise.

If you have specific preferences or interests, many tour operators offer customization options. You can often combine different tours to create a personalized itinerary, such as a guided city tour followed by a boat tour. Customization can help you focus on the aspects of Copenhagen that matter most to you and ensure a more tailored experience.

Choosing the right tour package for Copenhagen involves understanding the different types of tours available, considering your travel style and interests, and being mindful of seasonal variations. By doing your research and booking thoughtfully, you can find a tour that enhances your visit and helps you make the most of your time in this vibrant city.

Entry and visa requirements

Navigating entry and visa requirements can be a crucial step in planning your trip to Copenhagen. Here's a comprehensive guide to help you understand what you need to do to ensure a smooth entry into Denmark.

To determine if you need a visa for Copenhagen, start by checking whether your home country is part of the Schengen Area. Denmark is a member of the Schengen Area, which allows for visa-free travel between member countries for short stays of up to 90 days within a 180-day period. If you're from a country outside the Schengen Area, you may need a Schengen visa to enter Denmark.

The Schengen visa is a common requirement for travelers from many non-European countries. It allows you to travel not only to Denmark but also to other Schengen countries. To find out if you need a visa, consult the official website of the Danish embassy or consulate in your home country or visit the Schengen visa information portal. This will provide the most accurate and current visa requirements based on your nationality.

If you determine that you need a Schengen visa, follow these steps to apply:

1. Determine the Type of Visa: For short stays (up to 90 days), you'll need a Schengen short-stay visa (Type C). If you plan to stay longer or for other specific purposes (like study or work), you may need a different type of visa.

2. Gather Required Documents: Prepare the following documents for your visa application:
- Passport: It should be valid for at least three months beyond your planned stay in Denmark.
- Visa Application Form: Complete the form available from the Danish embassy or consulate's website.
- Photographs: Recent passport-sized photos that meet the specific requirements.
- Travel Arrangements: Proof of flight bookings showing your entry and exit from Denmark.
- Accommodation Bookings: Evidence of where you'll be staying during your visit.
- Proof of Financial Means: Documentation showing that you have sufficient funds to cover your stay in Denmark. This can include bank statements, pay slips, or a letter from a sponsor.

3. Submit Your Application: Schedule an appointment with the Danish embassy or consulate or a visa application center in your area. Submit your application along with the required documents. Some countries may require you to attend an interview as part of the process.

4. Pay the Visa Fee: The fee for a Schengen visa is generally around €80 for adults and €40 for children. Check the exact amount and payment method with the embassy or visa center.

5. Wait for Processing: Visa processing times can vary, but it generally takes around 15 calendar days. Apply well in advance of your travel date to account for any potential delays.

6. Receive Your Visa: If approved, you will receive a visa sticker in your passport. Check that all details are correct and match your travel plans.

For practical tips:
- Start the visa application process early to allow ample time for any issues that might arise.
- Use official resources like embassy websites or the Schengen visa portal to get the most reliable information.
- Ensure that all required documents are complete and accurate to avoid delays or rejections.

To help you navigate this process, consider creating a checklist of required documents and steps to follow. This can serve as a useful tool to ensure that you don't miss any critical parts of the application.

Example scenarios can illustrate how different nationalities might approach the visa process. For instance:
- U.S. Citizens: Typically do not require a visa for short stays (up to 90 days) but must ensure their passport is valid for at least three months beyond their planned stay.
- Indian Citizens: Generally need a Schengen visa. They will need to submit detailed documentation including proof of financial means and travel arrangements.

Understanding and preparing for entry and visa requirements can make your trip to Copenhagen hassle-free. By following the steps outlined and using the provided tips, you'll be well on your way to enjoying your visit to this charming city.

CHAPTER 2.
GETTING TO COPENHAGEN

Arriving by Air: Copenhagen Airport (CPH)

When arriving in Copenhagen, you'll likely land at Copenhagen Airport, known as CPH. It's the largest airport in Denmark and serves as a major gateway to the city. Here's what you need to know about navigating the airport and getting to the city.

Copenhagen Airport is well-organized and modern, making it easy for travelers to find their way. As you disembark from your flight, follow the signs for immigration and baggage claim. The airport is divided into two terminals: Terminal 1 and Terminal 2. Most international flights, including those from the US, Europe, and other regions, arrive at Terminal 3, which is connected to Terminal 2.

After clearing immigration, if you have checked luggage, head to the baggage claim area. Monitors will display the flight number and carousel where your luggage will arrive. If you're traveling with just hand luggage, you can skip this step and proceed to the arrivals hall.

Once you've collected your bags, you'll enter the arrivals hall. Here, you'll find several options for transportation into Copenhagen. The airport is well-connected, and getting into the city is straightforward.

To reach the city center, the train is a convenient choice. The airport has its own train station located directly underneath Terminal 3. Trains to Copenhagen Central Station run frequently, and the journey takes about 15 minutes. Tickets can be purchased from vending machines or the ticket counter in the train station. Make sure to check the schedules and purchase a ticket before boarding.

Alternatively, you can take a taxi from the airport. Taxis are available outside the arrivals area. The ride to the city center usually takes around 20 minutes, depending on traffic. While taxis are more expensive than trains, they offer door-to-door convenience if you have a lot of luggage or prefer a more direct route.

For a more budget-friendly option, you can also use the airport buses. Bus services, like the Flybus, operate between the airport and various locations in the city. Buses are well-signed and the journey to the city center takes roughly 30 minutes. Tickets can be bought from machines at the bus stops or online.

If you're staying in Copenhagen for a longer period, consider renting a car. Several rental agencies are located at the airport, and you can arrange your rental in advance or upon arrival. Keep in mind that parking in the city center can be challenging and expensive, so it's worth planning ahead.

Copenhagen Airport also offers various services and amenities to make your arrival as smooth as possible. There are information desks where you can ask for help or advice about getting to the city or your next destination. You'll also find shops, restaurants, and currency exchange services to meet any immediate needs.

Arriving at Copenhagen Airport is a straightforward process. Whether you choose the train, taxi, bus, or car rental, getting into the city is easy and efficient. The airport is well-equipped to handle travelers, ensuring that your journey from the airport to the heart of Copenhagen is as smooth as possible.

Choosing The Best Flight

When selecting the best flights to Copenhagen, there are several key factors to consider to ensure you get a good deal and a comfortable journey. Here's a detailed guide to help you navigate your options.

Major Airlines and Routes
Several major airlines offer direct flights to Copenhagen Airport (CPH), making it relatively easy to reach the city from various parts of the world. Key airlines that operate direct flights include Scandinavian Airlines (SAS), which provides numerous daily flights from major hubs like New York, London, and Stockholm. Other notable airlines include Norwegian Air Shuttle, which often has budget-friendly options, and Lufthansa, offering routes from major German cities.

The flight duration varies depending on your departure city. For example, a direct flight from New York to Copenhagen typically takes around 8 hours, while flights from London are approximately 2 hours. Scandinavian Airlines often provides additional amenities such as complimentary snacks and in-flight entertainment, which can enhance your travel experience.

Finding the Best Deals

To find the best deals on flights to Copenhagen, consider booking your tickets well in advance, ideally several months before your intended travel dates. Being flexible with your travel dates can also help you secure better prices. Often, flights are cheaper if you fly mid-week rather than on weekends.

Utilize price comparison websites like Skyscanner or Google Flights to compare fares across different airlines. Setting fare alerts on these platforms can notify you when prices drop. Additionally, keep an eye out for airline sales and promotions, which can offer substantial discounts.

Seasonal Variations

Flight prices and availability can fluctuate based on the season. Typically, summer months (June through August) are high season in Copenhagen, leading to higher flight prices and increased demand. Conversely, traveling during the shoulder seasons, such as spring (April to May) and autumn (September to October), often results in lower fares and fewer crowds. Winter can be a bit quieter and cheaper, though the weather might be colder and less predictable.

Airport Fees and Taxes

When flying to Copenhagen, be aware that airport fees and taxes can add to your travel costs. These fees are usually included in your ticket price, but it's worth checking the final amount during booking. Some budget airlines might have additional charges for things like seat selection or priority boarding. To minimize these costs, consider opting for airlines that include these fees in their ticket prices or compare total costs across different airlines.

Baggage Policies
Baggage policies can vary significantly between airlines. Most major airlines include a standard allowance for carry-on luggage and checked baggage. For example, Scandinavian Airlines typically allows one carry-on bag and one personal item per passenger, with checked baggage available for an additional fee. Norwegian Air Shuttle often charges separately for checked baggage, so be sure to review the airline's baggage policy when booking your flight.

If you're traveling with oversized or additional luggage, check the airline's policies and fees in advance to avoid unexpected charges. Some airlines offer special rates for additional luggage or oversized items if booked in advance.

Travel Classes and Amenities
When choosing your flight, consider the different travel classes offered. Economy class is the most budget-friendly, providing basic amenities such as in-flight meals and entertainment. Premium economy offers a bit more comfort, with additional legroom and enhanced service. Business class and first class provide the highest level of comfort, including spacious seating, premium meals, and priority boarding. The

choice of travel class will depend on your budget and preference for comfort and services.

Booking Tips
When booking flights to Copenhagen, aim to book your tickets during the airline's sales period or when prices are low. Navigate airline websites carefully to compare options and check cancellation policies and travel insurance offers. Ensure that the flight times and dates align with your travel plans to avoid any changes.

Loyalty Programs
If you frequently travel, consider joining an airline's loyalty program. Programs from airlines like Scandinavian Airlines and Lufthansa offer rewards such as miles, which can be redeemed for future flights, upgrades, or other perks. Accumulating points through these programs can provide significant benefits and savings on future trips.

Choosing the best flight to Copenhagen involves considering several factors, including airlines, seasonal variations, and baggage policies. By researching your options, booking in advance, and understanding the different classes and amenities, you can find a flight that fits your needs and budget. Remember that careful planning and research will help you ensure a comfortable and cost-effective travel experience.

Copenhagen airport: Arrival and Orientation

Arriving at Copenhagen Airport, known as Kastrup Airport (CPH), is a smooth and welcoming experience. This modern airport is well-organized and designed to make your arrival as easy as possible.

As your plane descends, you'll notice the sleek, contemporary design of the airport. Once you touch down and disembark, you'll follow signs to the baggage claim area if you have checked luggage. The airport's layout is straightforward, with clear signs in English and Danish, making it easy to navigate.

After collecting your luggage, proceed through customs. Depending on your nationality, you might need to show your passport and possibly your visa. The process is generally quick and efficient. If you're unsure about any paperwork or have questions, there are friendly staff members available to assist you.

Once you've cleared customs, you'll enter the arrivals hall. Here, you'll find various services to help you get started on your trip. There are information desks where you can ask about transportation options and get maps of the city. The airport also has currency exchange counters and ATMs if you need to withdraw Danish kroner.

For getting to the city center, you have several convenient options. The train station is located directly beneath the airport, and trains to Copenhagen Central Station take about 15 minutes. There are also buses that can take you to different parts of the city. If you prefer a taxi, you'll find a taxi stand right outside the arrivals hall. Taxis are a bit more expensive, but they offer door-to-door convenience.

If you're looking for a rental car, there are several rental agencies located at the airport. This can be a good option if you plan to explore beyond Copenhagen. For public transportation, you can purchase tickets at the airport's convenience stores or ticket machines. The trains and buses are reliable and offer a great way to see the city as you travel.

Copenhagen Airport is known for its cleanliness and efficiency. The airport also has a range of shops, cafes, and restaurants where you can grab a bite to eat or pick up any essentials before heading into the city.

Overall, arriving at Copenhagen Airport is a hassle-free experience. The airport's modern facilities and clear signage help make your transition from your flight to exploring the city smooth and easy.

Journey To Copenhagen

Making your way to Copenhagen is a straightforward and enjoyable experience, whether you're arriving by air, train, or car. Here's a guide to help you navigate your journey to this charming city.

If you're flying into Copenhagen, you'll land at Kastrup Airport (CPH), which is the main international gateway. The airport is well-connected to the city center. Once you arrive, you'll find clear signs directing you to various transportation options. The easiest way to get to downtown Copenhagen is by train. The train station is conveniently located right beneath the airport. Trains to Copenhagen Central Station run frequently and take about 15 minutes. Tickets can be bought at the airport's ticket machines or counters.

Alternatively, buses also connect the airport to various parts of the city. If you prefer a taxi, there's a taxi stand just outside the arrivals hall. Taxis offer door-to-door service but are more expensive compared to public transport. For those looking to rent a car, there are rental agencies at the airport. This might be a good option if you plan to explore the surrounding areas or if you're traveling with a group.

If you're traveling by train from other parts of Denmark or neighboring countries, Copenhagen Central Station is your main destination. It's well connected to the city and is a hub for both regional and international trains. The station is located in the heart of the city, making it easy to access public transportation, taxis, or even walk to many nearby attractions.

Driving to Copenhagen is also an option if you prefer to explore at your own pace. The city is well-connected by highways, and there are several parking options available. However, keep in mind that parking in central Copenhagen can be challenging and costly. It's often easier to use public transportation once you're in the city.

Regardless of how you arrive, Copenhagen's well-organized transport system and friendly locals will make your journey smooth and pleasant. The city is designed to be accessible, with clear signs and efficient services to help you find your way quickly. Whether you're arriving by air, train, or car, you'll be greeted by the welcoming charm of Copenhagen, ready to start your adventure in this vibrant city.

Arriving by Train: International and Domestic Connections

Arriving in Copenhagen by train is a smooth and pleasant experience, whether you're coming from nearby cities in Denmark or traveling from international destinations. The main hub for trains in Copenhagen is the Central Station, located right in the heart of the city. This central location makes it easy to access various parts of Copenhagen upon your arrival.

If you're traveling from within Denmark, you'll likely arrive at Copenhagen Central Station on a regional or intercity train. The trains are frequent, comfortable, and well-maintained. The journey from major Danish cities like Aarhus or Odense to Copenhagen takes a few hours and offers scenic views of the Danish countryside. Once you arrive at the station, you'll find a variety of services including shops, cafes, and ticket counters, which can make your arrival more convenient.

For international travelers, Copenhagen Central Station is also well-connected. If you're coming from countries like Sweden or Germany, you might arrive on an international train such as the Øresundståg from Malmö or the Intercity Express (ICE) from Hamburg. These trains are designed for comfort and efficiency, and the journey usually includes modern amenities to make your trip pleasant.

When you arrive at the Central Station, you'll find it easy to navigate. The station is equipped with clear signage in English, and there are several options for continuing your journey within the city. You can catch a local train, bus, or metro from the station. The local train network is extensive and can take you to various neighborhoods in Copenhagen. Additionally, the metro station is directly connected to the Central Station, providing quick access to different parts of the city and to the airport.

For those who prefer a more personalized approach, taxis and bike rentals are readily available at the station. If you're staying in the city for a while, it might be worth picking up a Copenhagen Card or city pass at the station. These passes often offer discounts on local attractions and public transport, making your stay even more enjoyable.

Overall, arriving by train in Copenhagen is a convenient and stress-free option. The Central Station's central location and excellent connections make it easy to start exploring the city right away. Whether you're arriving from within Denmark or from abroad, the train offers a comfortable and efficient way to reach Copenhagen.

Arriving by Bus

Arriving in Copenhagen by bus is a practical and cost-effective way to travel, especially if you're coming from nearby cities or other European destinations. Copenhagen's main bus terminal, known as the Ingerslevsgade bus terminal, is conveniently located close to the city center.

If you're traveling from within Denmark or from neighboring countries, you might arrive at this terminal, which is well-connected to the rest of the city. International bus services like FlixBus and Eurolines frequently operate routes to Copenhagen from various locations in Europe. These buses are comfortable and often offer amenities like Wi-Fi and power outlets, making your journey pleasant and connected.

Upon arrival at the bus terminal, you'll find that the area is equipped with basic facilities to make your experience smoother. There are often ticket counters where you can get information and purchase tickets for local transport. There are also shops and cafes nearby where you can grab a bite to eat or get refreshments.

The bus terminal is well-connected to the rest of Copenhagen. You can easily catch a local bus or train from the terminal to reach your destination within the city. The terminal is close to Copenhagen Central Station, so you can transfer to the train or metro services if needed. The local public transportation system is efficient, with frequent buses and trains that will help you get to various parts of the city quickly.

For convenience, it might be helpful to get a Copenhagen Card or city pass upon arrival. These passes offer discounts on local attractions and public transport, which can enhance your travel experience.

If you prefer a more personalized option, taxis and bike rentals are available near the terminal. Taxis can take you directly to your accommodation or any specific location in the city, while bike rentals are a great way to explore Copenhagen's scenic streets and canals.

Overall, arriving by bus in Copenhagen is a straightforward and affordable option. The terminal's close proximity to the city center and its connections to local transport make it easy to start exploring Copenhagen right away. Whether you're arriving from within Denmark or from further afield, traveling by bus offers a comfortable and economical way to reach the city.

Arriving by Sea: Ferry and Cruise Options

Arriving in Copenhagen by sea is a unique and scenic way to reach the city, offering a picturesque approach that sets the tone for your visit. Copenhagen is well-connected by both ferry services and cruise lines, making it an accessible destination from various locations.

If you're arriving by ferry, you'll likely dock at the Copenhagen Harbour, specifically at the DFDS Seaways terminal. DFDS Seaways operates ferry routes between Copenhagen and several other cities, including Oslo and Newcastle. The terminal is conveniently located close to the city center, so you can easily access transportation options to get to your final destination. After disembarking, you can catch a local bus or train, or even take a short walk to nearby attractions and accommodations.

For cruise travelers, Copenhagen serves as a major port for many cruise lines. The most common arrival point is the Langelinie Pier, which is situated in a beautiful part of the city with views of the iconic Little Mermaid statue. If you're arriving by cruise, you'll find that the pier is well-equipped with facilities to make your arrival smooth. There are information desks, taxis, and car rental services available right at the pier. The pier is also close to the city's central attractions, making it easy to start exploring right away.

Both ferry and cruise arrivals provide a wonderful introduction to Copenhagen's maritime charm. The harbor areas are often bustling with activity and offer stunning views of the city's waterfront and architectural landmarks. As you arrive, you might notice the mix of modern and historic buildings along the waterfront, creating a captivating first impression of Copenhagen.

When planning your arrival by sea, it's useful to check the schedule and book your tickets in advance, especially during peak tourist seasons. This ensures a smooth journey and helps you secure the best rates. Also, consider looking into any additional amenities or services offered by your ferry or cruise line to enhance your travel experience.

In summary, arriving by sea provides a memorable start to your Copenhagen adventure. Whether you're taking a ferry or arriving on a cruise, the city's accessible ports and scenic waterfront make it easy to dive right into exploring all that Copenhagen has to offer.

Getting Around: Public Transportation, Cycling, and Walking

Getting around Copenhagen is a breeze thanks to its well-organized public transportation system, the city's love for cycling, and its walkable streets. Each of these options offers a convenient and enjoyable way to explore the city.

Public transportation in Copenhagen is efficient and reliable. The city has an extensive network of buses, trains, and metro lines that can take you to almost any destination you might want to visit. The metro system is particularly handy, with lines that connect key areas of the city including the airport and central stations. Buses cover more localized routes and can get you closer to specific neighborhoods and attractions. The train system connects Copenhagen with other cities and towns in Denmark, as well as some international destinations. To use public transport, you can purchase a travel card or a single ticket. The travel cards are useful if you plan to use public transportation frequently, while single tickets are good for occasional rides. Tickets can be bought from machines at stations or through a mobile app.

Cycling is another popular and practical way to get around Copenhagen. The city is famous for its bike-friendly infrastructure, with dedicated bike lanes and plenty of bike parking. Renting a bike is straightforward; there are numerous bike rental shops and bike-sharing programs available throughout the city. Cycling allows you to explore Copenhagen at your own pace and is a great way to see both well-known sights and hidden gems. The city's flat terrain makes cycling easy, even for those who aren't regular cyclists.

Walking is also a great option, especially in central Copenhagen where many of the main attractions are close to each other. The city is designed to be pedestrian-friendly, with many areas where you can stroll comfortably and enjoy the charming streets and scenic views. Walking lets you fully experience the city's atmosphere and discover quirky shops, cozy cafes, and beautiful parks that you might miss if you were using other modes of transportation.

Overall, Copenhagen's public transportation, cycling options, and walkability make it easy to get around and enjoy everything the city has to offer. Whether you prefer to ride the metro, pedal through the streets, or take leisurely walks, you'll find that getting from one place to another is both simple and pleasant.

CHAPTER 3.
ACCOMMODATION OPTION

Finding the right place to stay in Copenhagen can greatly enhance your travel experience. Here's a detailed guide to help you choose the best accommodation for your needs, covering luxury hotels, boutique hotels, budget-friendly options, apartment rentals, and family-friendly stays.

Luxury Hotels: Opulent Stays in the City
Copenhagen's luxury hotels offer an exceptional level of comfort and service, perfect for those seeking a lavish experience. These hotels typically feature high-end amenities such as gourmet dining, spa services, and elegant rooms with stunning views.

1. Hotel d'Angleterre
Address: Kongens Nytorv 34, 1050 Copenhagen K, Denmark
Getting There: Located in the heart of the city, you can easily reach Hotel d'Angleterre by walking from Kongens Nytorv metro station or by taking a short taxi ride from Copenhagen Central Station.
Overview: This iconic hotel offers luxury in a historic setting with beautifully decorated rooms, a spa, and gourmet dining.
Booking Tips: Book well in advance, especially during peak tourist seasons, to secure the best rates. Look out for exclusive deals on their website or through high-end travel agencies.

2. Nimb Hotel
Address: Bernstorffsgade 5, 1577 Copenhagen, Denmark

Getting There: Situated within Tivoli Gardens, you can access Nimb Hotel from Tivoli Gardens' entrance or by a short walk from Copenhagen Central Station.

Overview: Nimb Hotel combines luxury with a whimsical atmosphere, offering unique rooms, a beautiful garden, and exquisite dining options.

Booking Tips: Check for seasonal promotions or package deals on their official website. Early booking is recommended for special events or holiday seasons.

3. Skt. Petri

Address: Krystalgade 22, 1172 Copenhagen, Denmark

Getting There: Located near Nørreport Station, Skt. Petri is easily accessible via the metro or a short walk from the train station.

Overview: This modern luxury hotel provides stylish accommodations, a rooftop terrace with panoramic city views, and an on-site restaurant.

Booking Tips: Look for special offers and book early to take advantage of the best rates and room upgrades.

Boutique Hotels: Stylish and Unique

Boutique hotels in Copenhagen are known for their distinctive character and personalized service. These hotels often feature unique designs and offer a more intimate experience compared to larger chains.

1. Hotel SP34

Address: Sankt Peders Stræde 34, 1453 Copenhagen K, Denmark

Getting There: Located in the Latin Quarter, you can reach Hotel SP34 by a short walk from Rådhuspladsen or via Nørreport Station.
Overview: This boutique hotel boasts a chic design with modern amenities, a cozy lounge, and a restaurant serving Nordic cuisine.
Booking Tips: Check their website for exclusive offers and book during the shoulder seasons for better rates.

2. Hotel Sanders
Address: Tirstræde 15, 1158 Copenhagen, Denmark
Getting There: Situated close to Kongens Nytorv, you can easily walk to Hotel Sanders from the metro station or take a short taxi ride from Copenhagen Central Station.
Overview: Known for its elegant decor and attentive service, Hotel Sanders offers a comfortable and stylish stay with a focus on personalized guest experiences.
Booking Tips: Book directly through their website for the best rates and additional perks. Look for special packages and seasonal promotions.

3. The Oddsson
Address: Grandi 5, 150 Reykjavik, Iceland
Getting There: Located in Reykjavik, Iceland, The Oddsson is accessible via local buses or a short taxi ride from Reykjavik's main attractions.
Overview: This hotel stands out with its quirky design and modern amenities, offering a unique experience in Reykjavik.
Booking Tips: Check for discounts and book in advance, especially during peak travel times.

Budget-Friendly Options: Hostels and Affordable Stays

For travelers seeking budget-friendly options, Copenhagen offers several hostels and affordable accommodations. These are ideal for those looking to save money while still enjoying a comfortable stay.

1. Steel House Copenhagen

Address: Herholdtsgade 6, 1605 Copenhagen, Denmark
Getting There: Located near the central train station, you can reach Steel House Copenhagen by walking from Copenhagen Central Station or taking a short metro ride.
Overview: This modern hostel features clean, comfortable rooms, a bar, and a common area with games and activities.
Booking Tips: Look for deals on hostel booking sites and consider booking a dormitory-style room for lower rates.

2. City Hub Copenhagen

Address: Nansensgade 45, 1366 Copenhagen, Denmark
Getting There: A short walk from Nørreport Station, City Hub Copenhagen is easily accessible by metro or bus.
Overview: Offering a unique capsule-style accommodation, City Hub provides privacy at an affordable price with modern amenities.
Booking Tips: Book in advance and use comparison websites to find the best rates. Check for special discounts on their website.

3. Copenhagen Downtown Hostel

Address: Vandkunsten 5, 1665 Copenhagen, Denmark

Getting There: Located in the city center, this hostel is within walking distance from Rådhuspladsen and Copenhagen Central Station.
Overview: A popular choice for budget travelers, it offers dormitory-style rooms, a bar, and organized social events.
Booking Tips: Book early for the best rates and look for promotions on hostel booking platforms.

Apartment Rentals: Live Like a Local
Renting an apartment can offer a home-like experience and flexibility, ideal for longer stays or those who prefer self-catering.

1. Airbnb - Central Copenhagen Apartments
Address: Varies by listing
Getting There: Use the Airbnb app or website to find apartments throughout central Copenhagen. Most are easily reachable via public transportation.
Overview: Airbnb offers a range of options from cozy studios to larger apartments with full kitchens, allowing you to live like a local.
Booking Tips: Book early, especially during peak travel seasons, and read reviews to ensure quality. Look for properties with high ratings and good host feedback.

2. Copenhagen Apartments
Address: Varies by listing
Getting There: Check listings on platforms like Booking.com or local rental websites. Many apartments are accessible via public transportation.

Overview: Offers various apartment sizes and styles across the city, providing flexibility in accommodation choices.
Booking Tips: Compare different rental platforms and book well in advance. Check for discounts and long-term stay options.

3. Sonder - Kødbyen Apartments
Address: Varies by listing
Getting There: Located in the trendy Vesterbro district, these apartments are accessible by metro and bus.
Overview: Sonder offers stylish, fully-equipped apartments with modern amenities in vibrant neighborhoods.
Booking Tips: Look for deals on their website and consider booking a longer stay for better rates.

Family-Friendly Accommodations
For families, finding accommodations with kid-friendly amenities and spacious rooms is key.

1. Tivoli Hotel & Congress Center
Address: Arni Magnussons Gade 2, 1577 Copenhagen, Denmark
Getting There: Located next to Tivoli Gardens, easily reachable from Copenhagen Central Station or via a short metro ride.
Overview: This hotel offers family rooms, a pool, and proximity to Tivoli Gardens, making it ideal for families.
Booking Tips: Book early, especially during peak vacation periods, and check for family packages that include tickets to Tivoli Gardens.

2. Crowne Plaza Copenhagen Towers

Address: Copenhagen Towers, Ørestads Boulevard 114-118, 2300 Copenhagen S, Denmark

Getting There: Easily accessible via the metro from Copenhagen Central Station or a short drive from the airport.

Overview: This hotel provides spacious family rooms, a kids' play area, and green spaces nearby.

Booking Tips: Look for special offers and family-friendly packages on their website. Book in advance to secure the best rates.

3. CABINN Metro Hotel

Address: Arne Jacobsens Allé 2, 2300 Copenhagen S, Denmark

Getting There: Located near the Bella Center Metro Station, accessible by metro from the city center and a short walk to the hotel.

Overview: Offers budget-friendly family rooms with basic amenities and easy access to public transportation.

Booking Tips: Book early and check for family room discounts. Use comparison websites to find the best deals.

Comparative Analysis

When choosing accommodation in Copenhagen, consider what best suits your needs. Luxury hotels provide high-end amenities and prime locations but come at a higher cost. Boutique hotels offer unique experiences and stylish decor but might be pricier than budget options. Budget-friendly hostels and affordable stays are great for saving money but might have fewer amenities. Apartment rentals offer flexibility and a local experience but require more planning. Family-friendly accommodations cater specifically to families with children and often provide additional amenities, though they may be pricier.

Copenhagen offers a wide range of accommodation options to suit various preferences and budgets. Whether you're seeking luxury, a unique boutique experience, affordable lodging, a home-like stay, or family-friendly options, you'll find something that fits your needs. Make sure to book in advance, check for deals, and consider what amenities are important for a comfortable stay.

CHAPTER 4.
NEIGHBORHOOD OF COPENHAGEN

Indre By: The Historic Heart of Copenhagen

Indre By, often referred to as the historic heart of Copenhagen, is a vibrant and charming area that embodies the city's rich history and culture. When you explore Indre By, you'll find yourself wandering through streets that have witnessed centuries of history, from royal palaces to bustling markets.

As you walk through Indre By, you'll be surrounded by some of Copenhagen's most iconic landmarks. The area is home to the stunning Amalienborg Palace, where the Danish royal family resides. The palace complex consists of four identical buildings arranged around an octagonal courtyard. It's a great spot to catch the changing of the guard ceremony, which takes place daily and is a fascinating glimpse into Danish royal traditions.

Nearby, you'll discover the famous Nyhavn, a picturesque waterfront lined with colorful 17th-century townhouses and lively restaurants. This area was once a busy port but is now a favorite spot for both locals and tourists. You can take a leisurely stroll along the canal, enjoy a meal at one of the outdoor cafes, or even hop on a canal boat tour to see the city from the water.

Another must-visit in Indre By is the Strøget, one of Europe's longest pedestrian streets. This bustling shopping avenue is lined with a mix of high-end boutiques, international brands, and charming local shops. It's also home to some historic buildings, including the beautiful Rådhus (City Hall) with its impressive tower offering panoramic views of the city.

For a dose of culture, the National Museum of Denmark is a treasure trove of exhibits showcasing the country's history, from the Vikings to the present day. The museum is housed in a grand building and provides a deep dive into Danish heritage and artifacts.

If you're interested in architectural marvels, be sure to visit the Round Tower (Rundetårn), an iconic 17th-century observatory with a unique spiral ramp leading to the top. The views from the top are spectacular, offering a bird's-eye view of the city and its rooftops.

Indre By is also home to the Church of Our Lady (Vor Frue Kirke), the cathedral of Copenhagen. This church, with its impressive neoclassical design, houses several important sculptures and is known for its serene and grand interior.

When it comes to dining, Indre By offers a diverse range of options. From traditional Danish smørrebrød (open-faced sandwiches) to modern cuisine, there's something to suit every palate. Many restaurants offer outdoor seating, allowing you to enjoy the lively street scenes and picturesque views.

Getting around Indre By is easy, as the area is compact and walkable. Many of the attractions and landmarks are within walking distance of each other. You'll also find plenty of bike rental stations if you prefer to explore by bicycle.

Indre By is a vibrant and historic district that captures the essence of Copenhagen. With its rich history, beautiful architecture, and lively streets, it offers a delightful experience for anyone interested in exploring the heart of Denmark's capital. Whether you're taking in the sights, enjoying the food, or simply soaking up the atmosphere, Indre By is a must-visit destination that embodies the charm and history of Copenhagen.

Vesterbro: The Trendy and Bohemian District

Vesterbro is a vibrant and eclectic district in Copenhagen known for its trendy and bohemian atmosphere. Once a gritty area with a rough edge, it has transformed into one of the city's most exciting neighborhoods, brimming with creative energy and a youthful vibe.

As you wander through Vesterbro, you'll immediately notice the lively streets filled with an array of unique shops, cozy cafes, and cutting-edge restaurants. The district is known for its creative flair, and you'll see this reflected in the colorful street art and stylish boutiques that line the avenues.

One of the central spots in Vesterbro is the Meatpacking District (Kødbyen), an area that has been revitalized from its industrial past into a bustling hub of food and culture. Here, you'll find an impressive range of restaurants and bars offering everything from gourmet dining to casual street food. The Meatpacking District is especially lively in the evenings, with many places hosting live music and events that draw locals and visitors alike.

Another highlight in Vesterbro is the Tivoli Gardens amusement park, though technically on the edge of the district. This historic park, which dates back to 1843, is a must-visit for its charming blend of classic rides, beautifully landscaped gardens, and seasonal events. It's a place where you can experience the magic of Copenhagen, whether you're enjoying the rides, catching a show, or simply strolling through the enchanting surroundings.

For those who appreciate a good coffee or a relaxing place to unwind, Vesterbro has numerous charming cafes. These spots often double as art galleries or performance spaces, reflecting the district's artistic spirit. The cafes here are known for their unique decor, great coffee, and relaxed ambiance, making them perfect for a leisurely break.

Vesterbro is also home to a number of cool and creative spaces like the Copenhagen Contemporary art center, which showcases contemporary art in a dynamic setting. It's a place where you can explore innovative exhibitions and engage with modern art in an interactive way.

If you're a fan of vintage shopping, Vesterbro has several second-hand and antique stores where you can find everything from retro clothing to quirky home decor. These shops are perfect for finding unique items and experiencing the district's eclectic style.

The local vibe in Vesterbro is very welcoming and friendly. The residents are often seen enjoying the outdoor spaces, such as the popular Enghave Park, a green oasis in the middle of the bustling city. It's a great spot for a picnic, a jog, or just a relaxing afternoon with locals.

Getting around Vesterbro is easy, as the district is well-connected by public transport and bike lanes. The area is bike-friendly, and many visitors and locals choose to explore by bike, allowing for an enjoyable and efficient way to see the sights.

Vesterbro is a lively and creative district that offers a unique and engaging experience in Copenhagen. With its trendy vibe, diverse dining options, artistic spaces, and friendly atmosphere, it's a great place to explore and soak up the vibrant culture of the city. Whether you're looking for great food, interesting shops, or just a place to relax and enjoy the local scene, Vesterbro has something special to offer.

Nørrebro: Multicultural and Vibrant

Nørrebro is one of Copenhagen's most multicultural and vibrant neighborhoods, full of energy and diversity. As you step into Nørrebro, you'll be struck by the lively streets and the mix of cultures that give the area its unique character.

The district is known for its rich cultural tapestry, reflected in the variety of restaurants, shops, and markets that line its streets. Walking through Nørrebro, you'll encounter a blend of international cuisines, from Middle Eastern and African to Asian and European, offering a true taste of the neighborhood's global influence.

One of the key attractions in Nørrebro is the Superkilen Park, a remarkable public space designed to celebrate diversity. The park is divided into three distinct sections—The Red Square, The Black Market, and The Green Park—each featuring different elements that represent various cultures. You'll find colorful playgrounds, unique sculptures, and even an outdoor gym. It's a wonderful place to explore and experience the neighborhood's artistic and cultural spirit.

Another highlight is the Assistens Cemetery, a historic and serene spot where many notable figures, including Hans Christian Andersen, are buried. It's not just a cemetery but also a tranquil park where locals and visitors come to stroll, relax, and enjoy the lush greenery. The cemetery is beautifully landscaped and provides a peaceful escape from the hustle and bustle of city life.

Nørrebro is also famous for its vibrant street life. The area around Nørrebrogade and Jægersborggade is particularly bustling, with a wide range of shops selling everything from vintage clothing and handmade crafts to international delicacies. Jægersborggade is especially known for its trendy cafes, artisan bakeries, and unique boutiques, making it a great spot for a leisurely stroll and some shopping.

The district has a lively cultural scene, with many galleries, theaters, and music venues. You might find yourself drawn to the many events and performances happening throughout the year, showcasing everything from local music and theater to international artists.

For those interested in local markets, Nørrebro offers a vibrant selection of options. The Nørrebro Flea Market is a popular spot where you can browse through a variety of second-hand goods, antiques, and vintage finds. It's a great place to hunt for unique items and enjoy the lively atmosphere of the market.

Nørrebro is also known for its community spirit. The area is home to many local initiatives and projects that reflect the diversity and creativity of its residents. You might come across community events, cultural festivals, and art exhibitions that showcase the rich mix of cultures and talents in the neighborhood.

Getting around Nørrebro is easy with its well-connected public transport options, including buses and trains. The area is also bike-friendly, so you can explore its many attractions on two wheels if you prefer.

In summary, Nørrebro is a dynamic and multicultural district that offers a vibrant and diverse experience in Copenhagen. With its rich array of restaurants, cultural landmarks, unique shops, and lively street life, it's a fantastic place to explore and immerse yourself in the city's diverse culture. Whether you're looking for great food, interesting shops, or a taste of local life, Nørrebro has something special to offer.

Østerbro: Chic and Family-Friendly

Østerbro is a charming and family-friendly district in Copenhagen, known for its chic atmosphere and relaxed vibe. As you wander through Østerbro, you'll quickly notice the neighborhood's blend of stylish living and laid-back charm, making it a great choice for families and those seeking a more tranquil experience.

One of the standout features of Østerbro is its beautiful parks and green spaces. The largest and most popular is Fælledparken, a vast park that offers plenty of space for outdoor activities. It's perfect for picnics, playing sports, or simply taking a leisurely stroll. The park has playgrounds for children, a large pond, and even a skate park, making it a favorite spot for families.

Another lovely spot is Østre Anlæg, a picturesque park that's ideal for a relaxing afternoon. With its winding paths, serene lakes, and abundant greenery, it provides a peaceful retreat from the urban hustle. It's also home to the Hirschsprung Collection, a museum featuring Danish art from the 19th and early 20th centuries, which adds a cultural touch to your visit.

Østerbro is also known for its stylish shopping streets. Østerbrogade, the main thoroughfare, is lined with boutiques, cafes, and specialty shops. Here, you can find everything from high-end fashion to unique local goods. The area has a refined yet welcoming feel, making it enjoyable to explore and shop.

If you're a fan of local markets, the Torvehallerne market is worth a visit. Located nearby, it offers a range of fresh produce, gourmet foods, and local delicacies. It's a great place to pick up some ingredients for a homemade meal or simply enjoy a delicious snack.

For families with young children, Østerbro has several family-friendly attractions. The Copenhagen Zoo, located in the nearby Frederiksberg area, is a short trip away and provides a fun and educational experience for kids of all ages. The zoo is home to a wide range of animals and features interactive exhibits and play areas.

In terms of dining, Østerbro offers a variety of options to suit different tastes and budgets. You'll find cozy cafes, trendy restaurants, and casual eateries serving everything from Danish comfort food to international cuisine. The area has a relaxed dining atmosphere, making it easy to find a spot to enjoy a meal with family or friends.

Getting around Østerbro is convenient, with excellent public transportation options including buses and trains. The area is also bike-friendly, with well-maintained cycling paths that make exploring the district easy and enjoyable.

Østerbro is a chic and family-friendly neighborhood that combines stylish living with a relaxed atmosphere. With its beautiful parks, charming shopping streets, and family-friendly attractions, it offers a pleasant and enjoyable experience for visitors of all ages. Whether you're looking to relax in a park, shop in boutique stores, or enjoy a meal in a cozy cafe, Østerbro provides a delightful and welcoming environment.

Christianshavn: Canals and Counterculture

Christianshavn is a unique and vibrant part of Copenhagen, known for its picturesque canals and distinctive counterculture vibe. This district offers a charming mix of historical charm and modern bohemian spirit, making it a fascinating place to explore.

One of the most striking features of Christianshavn is its beautiful canals. As you stroll along the water, you'll see colorful old buildings reflecting in the canals, creating a picturesque scene that's perfect for photos. The canals add a serene and scenic element to the area, making it a pleasant place for a leisurely walk or a relaxing boat ride.

One of the highlights in Christianshavn is the Freetown Christiania, a self-proclaimed autonomous neighborhood that has become a symbol of counterculture. Christiania is known for its creative and alternative lifestyle, with colorful murals, unique architecture, and a lively arts scene. The area has a relaxed and welcoming atmosphere, and while it's a popular spot for visitors, it's also a living community with its own rules and customs. Exploring Christiania can be an eye-opening experience, offering insight into a different way of life and a chance to enjoy local art, crafts, and music.

Another notable site in Christianshavn is the Church of Our Saviour. This baroque church is famous for its corkscrew-shaped spire that offers panoramic views of the city from the top. Climbing the 400 steps to the top is a bit of a workout, but the breathtaking view of Copenhagen and the surrounding areas makes it worthwhile.

Christianshavn is also home to some great dining options. You'll find a variety of cafes and restaurants offering everything from traditional Danish dishes to international cuisine. Many eateries have a cozy and relaxed atmosphere, reflecting the district's unique character. If you're interested in trying some Danish specialties, look for places serving open-faced sandwiches or fresh seafood.

For a cultural experience, consider visiting the Danish Architecture Center, which is nearby. The center offers exhibitions and information about Danish architecture and urban design, providing insights into the city's development and architectural heritage.

Getting around Christianshavn is quite easy. The district is well-connected by public transportation, with several bus and metro lines passing through. It's also a pleasant area for walking or cycling, with many paths and trails making it easy to explore the local sights.

In summary, Christianshavn is a delightful district that blends historical charm with a vibrant and eclectic spirit. The scenic canals, unique counterculture of Christiania, and beautiful landmarks like the Church of Our Saviour make it a memorable part of Copenhagen. Whether you're exploring the colorful streets, enjoying a meal in a cozy cafe, or taking in the views from the church tower, Christianshavn offers a rich and enjoyable experience for visitors.

Frederiksberg: Green Spaces and Regal Charm

Frederiksberg is a charming and elegant part of Copenhagen known for its beautiful green spaces and regal atmosphere. This area stands out for its blend of lush parks, grand architecture, and a more relaxed pace, offering a different perspective of the city.

One of the most notable features of Frederiksberg is its extensive green spaces. The Frederiksberg Gardens, a sprawling park with serene lakes and historic buildings, is a highlight. It's a fantastic place to take a leisurely stroll, have a picnic, or just relax by the water. The park's landscape is dotted with charming bridges, statues, and tree-lined paths, creating a peaceful escape from the city's hustle and bustle. The gardens are also home to the Frederiksberg Palace, a grand historic building that adds a touch of regal charm to the surroundings.

Another green gem in Frederiksberg is the Copenhagen Zoo, which is one of the oldest zoos in Europe. The zoo is set within a spacious park and offers a pleasant day out for visitors of all ages. With a variety of animals, including elephants, lions, and pandas, the zoo is both educational and entertaining. The zoo's historic architecture and beautiful grounds enhance the overall experience, making it a favorite spot for families and nature enthusiasts.

Frederiksberg also boasts some impressive architecture. The area is known for its elegant buildings and historic mansions, reflecting a sense of old-world charm. Walking through Frederiksberg's streets, you'll encounter a mix of traditional and modern designs, with quaint cafes and boutique shops adding to the district's appeal.

For dining, Frederiksberg offers a range of options from cozy cafes to upscale restaurants. Many eateries feature outdoor seating, allowing you to enjoy a meal in a pleasant setting, especially during the warmer months. Whether you're in the mood for a casual brunch or a fine dining experience, you'll find plenty of choices in this district.

Shopping in Frederiksberg is also a treat. The area features a mix of high-end boutiques, specialty stores, and charming local shops. It's a great place to find unique gifts, stylish clothing, or simply enjoy a relaxed shopping experience.

Getting around Frederiksberg is easy and enjoyable. The area is well-served by public transportation, including buses and metro lines, making it convenient to reach from other parts of Copenhagen. Cycling is also a popular way to explore, with plenty of bike paths and bike rental options available.

Frederiksberg offers a delightful blend of green spaces, elegant architecture, and a relaxed atmosphere. The Frederiksberg Gardens and Copenhagen Zoo provide beautiful settings for relaxation and family outings, while the district's charming streets and dining options add to its appeal. Whether you're wandering through the parks, enjoying a meal at a local cafe, or exploring the elegant buildings, Frederiksberg is a lovely part of Copenhagen that promises a serene and enjoyable experience.

Amager: The Emerging Area with a Beachside Vibe

Amager is an up-and-coming part of Copenhagen, known for its laid-back beachside vibe and modern development. It's a vibrant area that combines natural beauty with contemporary urban life, offering a unique experience for visitors.

One of Amager's main attractions is its beautiful coastline. The Amager Beach Park is a highlight, stretching along the eastern shore. This sandy beach is a favorite spot for locals and visitors alike. It's a perfect place for sunbathing, swimming, or taking a leisurely walk along the shore. There are also plenty of grassy areas where you can have a picnic or just relax and enjoy the views of the water. The beach park is well-equipped with facilities like cafes, playgrounds, and bike paths, making it a great spot for a day out.

Nearby, you'll find Amager Strandpark, another popular beach area with a mix of sandy and pebbly shores. It offers excellent opportunities for water sports, including windsurfing and kayaking. The park is a pleasant place for outdoor activities and enjoying Copenhagen's coastal atmosphere.

Amager is also known for its modern and stylish architecture. The area has seen significant development in recent years, with new residential buildings, shops, and restaurants popping up. The district's urban landscape features sleek, contemporary designs that contrast with Copenhagen's historic architecture, creating a dynamic and exciting environment.

For dining, Amager has a range of options, from trendy cafes to casual eateries. The area's culinary scene is diverse, offering everything from international cuisine to local Danish specialties. Many restaurants and cafes have outdoor seating, allowing you to enjoy your meal while taking in the beachside ambiance.

Shopping in Amager is a mix of local boutiques and larger retail stores. The area has several shopping centers and malls, providing a variety of shopping experiences. Whether you're looking for unique local finds or just browsing, Amager's shopping options are worth exploring.

Getting around Amager is straightforward. The area is well-served by public transportation, including buses and metro lines, which connect it to the rest of Copenhagen. Biking is also popular, with dedicated bike paths making it easy to explore the district and enjoy its scenic coastal views.

In summary, Amager offers a refreshing blend of beachside relaxation and modern urban living. With its beautiful beaches, contemporary architecture, and diverse dining and shopping options, it's an exciting area to explore. Whether you're spending a day at the beach, enjoying a meal at a local cafe, or simply strolling through the district, Amager provides a unique and enjoyable experience in Copenhagen.

CHAPTER 5.
TOP ATTRACTION

The Little Mermaid: Copenhagen's Iconic Symbol

The Little Mermaid is a beloved icon of Copenhagen, nestled by the waterfront in Langelinie Park. This statue, inspired by Hans Christian Andersen's famous fairy tale, has become one of the most recognizable symbols of the city. As I visited the statue, I was struck by how its understated charm captivated both locals and tourists alike.

The statue sits on a rock in the harbor, looking out over the water. Despite its small size, about 1.25 meters tall, it has an undeniable presence. I found it particularly enchanting as I approached from the park's pathways, where the gentle sea breeze and the distant sounds of the city created a serene atmosphere. The simplicity of the statue contrasted beautifully with the bustling city around it, offering a peaceful retreat by the water.

To reach The Little Mermaid, I took a pleasant walk from the city center. If you're using public transport, it's easy to catch a bus or a train that will get you close to the park. The nearest metro station is Østerport, from where it's a short walk to Langelinie Park. Alternatively, a scenic stroll from the city center takes you through some lovely parts of Copenhagen, allowing you to enjoy the city's charm along the way.

The address for The Little Mermaid is Langelinie, 2100 Copenhagen, Denmark. It's in a picturesque park area with lovely views of the harbor, making the visit even more enjoyable. The park itself is free to enter, and so is the statue, which is a pleasant surprise for many visitors. There are no fees to view The Little Mermaid, and you can spend as much time as you like admiring it.

To make the most of your visit, consider arriving early in the day to avoid the larger crowds that tend to gather later. The morning light can be particularly beautiful, casting a gentle glow over the statue and the surrounding water. If you're a fan of photography, the early hours offer a great opportunity for capturing the statue without too many people in the frame.

While at the statue, take a moment to enjoy the surrounding park. Langelinie Park is a lovely place for a relaxing stroll, with ample green space and well-maintained paths. You might also want to explore the nearby harbor area, which offers scenic views and a few cafes where you can enjoy a coffee or snack while taking in the atmosphere.

My experience visiting The Little Mermaid was quite memorable. It was a simple yet profound reminder of the magic that a story can create, brought to life in the heart of Copenhagen. The statue's tranquil setting provided a perfect spot for reflection and a wonderful photo opportunity. Whether you're a fan of Andersen's tales or just looking to enjoy a peaceful moment by the water, The Little Mermaid is a must-see highlight of Copenhagen.

Tivoli Gardens: The World's Second-Oldest Amusement Park

Tivoli Gardens stands as a charming and historic amusement park nestled in the heart of Copenhagen. As I wandered through its gates, I was instantly captivated by the blend of old-world enchantment and modern thrill that defines this place. Established in 1843, it's the world's second-oldest amusement park and remains a beloved attraction for both locals and visitors.

The park is located at Vesterbrogade 3, 1630 Copenhagen, Denmark. Getting there is quite straightforward. If you're coming from the city center, it's a short walk away, or you can hop on the nearby metro. The Nørreport and Tivoli Gardens stations are both convenient, with the latter putting you right at the entrance. Buses also frequent the area, making it easy to find your way to this magical spot.

Tivoli Gardens is not free to enter. The entrance fee grants access to the park's grounds, which are beautifully landscaped and feature an array of gardens, fountains, and enchanting architecture. As of my visit, the entrance fee was around 135 DKK for adults, with reduced prices for children and seniors. For an additional cost, you can purchase tickets for individual rides or opt for an unlimited ride pass, which offers great value if you plan to try out several attractions.

What I found particularly delightful was how Tivoli Gardens combines classic amusement park rides with beautiful, seasonal decor. The park transforms throughout the year, each season bringing its own unique charm. During my visit, the summer months brought vibrant flower displays and a lively atmosphere, while the winter season promised a magical Christmas market with twinkling lights and festive treats.

To make the most of your visit, I recommend starting early in the day to enjoy the park before it gets too crowded. Strolling through the park, you can explore its various themed areas, from the whimsical fairy-tale-inspired rides to the more exhilarating roller coasters. Tivoli Gardens is known for its beautiful architecture, so be sure to take some time to admire the intricate details of its historic buildings and the impressive central carousel.

In addition to the rides, Tivoli Gardens offers a variety of dining options, ranging from casual eateries to fine dining restaurants. I had a wonderful time enjoying a meal at one of the park's outdoor cafes, where I could savor a delicious Danish pastry while soaking in the lively atmosphere. There are also numerous stands and kiosks offering everything from hot dogs to sweet treats, perfect for a quick bite as you explore.

For those interested in entertainment, Tivoli Gardens features a diverse lineup of shows and performances. From live music and theatrical performances to seasonal events, there's always something happening in the park. Be sure to check the schedule in advance so you can plan your visit around any special events or performances that might interest you.

My visit to Tivoli Gardens was a delightful experience, blending nostalgia with modern fun in a beautifully maintained setting. Whether you're a thrill-seeker or simply looking for a picturesque place to wander and relax, Tivoli Gardens offers a little something for everyone. Its rich history and vibrant atmosphere make it a standout attraction in Copenhagen, well worth a visit.

Nyhavn: The Colorful Waterfront and its History

Nyhavn, Copenhagen's iconic waterfront, is a vibrant slice of the city that I found absolutely irresistible. Nestled at Nyhavn 1-71, 1051 Copenhagen K, this charming district is famed for its colorful buildings, historic ships, and lively atmosphere. As soon as I arrived, I was captivated by the picturesque scene that has been a favorite among locals and tourists alike for centuries.

To get to Nyhavn, it's quite easy from various parts of Copenhagen. If you're staying in the city center, it's a pleasant walk through the heart of Copenhagen, taking you through some lovely streets and past notable landmarks. Alternatively, you can take the metro to Kongens Nytorv station, which is a short walk from Nyhavn. Several buses and even some canal tours stop nearby, making it convenient to reach from different parts of the city.

There is no entrance fee to explore Nyhavn itself, which is fantastic. You can wander along the waterfront, admire the colorful 17th-century houses, and enjoy the lively atmosphere without any cost. The real charm of Nyhavn lies in its open, free-access streets and waterways, making it an ideal spot for a leisurely stroll.

During my visit, I spent time soaking in the lively ambiance and admiring the stunning architecture. The buildings along Nyhavn are a rainbow of colors, creating a beautiful backdrop against the boats and the canal. Many of these historic buildings date back to the 17th century, and as I wandered along the waterfront, I felt a deep sense of connection to Copenhagen's rich maritime history.

One of the highlights of Nyhavn is the chance to explore its historic ships, which are docked along the canal. These old wooden boats add a unique charm to the waterfront, and some are even used for private charters and canal tours. I enjoyed taking a moment to admire these beautifully restored vessels and learn a bit about their history.

For dining, Nyhavn offers a range of options right along the waterfront. I treated myself to a meal at one of the many restaurants and cafes lining the canal. It was a delight to sit outside, enjoying a Danish open-faced sandwich while taking in the lively views of tourists and locals alike. The area is known for its seafood, so don't miss out on trying some fresh fish dishes if you're a fan of seafood.

There are also plenty of bars and cafes where you can enjoy a drink or a coffee while watching the world go by. It's a great spot to relax and take in the vibrant atmosphere of Copenhagen. The outdoor seating areas are perfect for people-watching and soaking up the sun, especially on a warm day.

Another must-do in Nyhavn is to take a canal tour. Several companies operate boat tours from the area, offering a unique perspective of the city from the water. I found this to be a fantastic way to see some of Copenhagen's key landmarks and learn more about the city's history from a different angle.

In the evening, Nyhavn transforms with a different charm as the lights reflect off the water and the atmosphere becomes even more enchanting. The area takes on a lively but relaxed vibe, perfect for an evening stroll or a leisurely dinner.

Overall, Nyhavn is a must-visit destination in Copenhagen. Its historical significance, beautiful setting, and vibrant atmosphere make it a place that truly captures the essence of the city. Whether you're strolling along the canal, enjoying a meal with a view, or taking a boat tour, Nyhavn offers a memorable experience that beautifully showcases Copenhagen's charm.

Rosenborg Castle: A Glimpse into Royal Life

Rosenborg Castle, a jewel in Copenhagen's crown, offers a fascinating glimpse into Denmark's royal history. Located at Slotsholmsgade 1, 1216 Copenhagen K, this castle is a splendid example of Renaissance architecture and a must-visit for anyone interested in royal life and history.

Reaching Rosenborg Castle is straightforward. If you're staying in central Copenhagen, it's a pleasant walk from many major landmarks. The castle is situated in the King's Garden (Kongens Have), which is a lovely park where you can enjoy a stroll before or after your visit. Alternatively, you can take the metro to Nørreport Station, which is about a ten-minute walk from the castle. Several buses also stop nearby, making it easy to access from various parts of the city.

As for entrance, Rosenborg Castle is a paid attraction. When I visited, the ticket cost was around 125 DKK for adults, with discounts available for children, students, and seniors. It's a good idea to check the official website or local tourist information for the most current pricing and any special promotions. The castle offers free entry on certain days or times, so it's worth checking their schedule if you're looking to visit on a budget.

Once you arrive, the castle's exterior alone is worth the visit. The red-brick façade, complete with a charming green copper roof, stands out beautifully against the park's greenery. The castle was originally built as a royal summer residence in the early 17th century and has been preserved as a museum showcasing Danish royal history.

Inside, the castle is a treasure trove of historical artifacts and royal regalia. I was immediately struck by the lavish interiors, with rooms decorated in exquisite period styles. The Great Hall, in particular, is breathtaking with its impressive collection of royal crowns, scepters, and the coronation regalia of Danish kings and queens. It's a chance to marvel at the opulence that defined royal life in Denmark centuries ago.

One of the highlights of the castle is the Crown Jewels and the Danish Crown Regalia. These are displayed in a special chamber that is both intriguing and awe-inspiring. The craftsmanship of the regalia is remarkable, and seeing these pieces up close gave me a profound sense of the history and tradition behind them.

The castle also houses the King's Gardens, a beautiful park where you can relax and enjoy a leisurely stroll. The gardens are meticulously maintained and provide a peaceful retreat from the hustle and bustle of the city. The well-manicured lawns and blooming flowers make it an ideal spot for a break, and the view of the castle from the gardens is picturesque.

A guided tour can enrich your visit. While wandering the rooms and halls is fascinating on its own, the additional insights from a knowledgeable guide offer a deeper understanding of the castle's history and its significance in Danish culture. Audio guides are also available for those who prefer exploring at their own pace.

To make the most of your visit, consider arriving early to avoid the crowds and to fully enjoy each exhibit without feeling rushed. The castle's compact size means you can explore it thoroughly in a few hours, making it a great addition to any day of sightseeing.

Rosenborg Castle offers an enchanting journey back in time, providing a window into the grandeur of Danish royalty. Its combination of stunning architecture, rich history, and beautiful surroundings makes it a standout attraction in Copenhagen. Whether you're captivated by royal history, intricate designs, or simply enjoy exploring historical landmarks, Rosenborg Castle is a memorable experience that beautifully captures the essence of Denmark's royal heritage.

Amalienborg Palace: The Royal Family's Winter Residence

Amalienborg Palace, situated at Amalienborg Slotsplads 5, 1257 Copenhagen K, is the regal winter residence of the Danish royal family. As I approached this grand ensemble of palaces, the sense of history and majesty was palpable. The palace complex is a striking example of Rococo architecture, with its four identical buildings arranged around an octagonal courtyard, each adding to the overall elegance of the site.

To reach Amalienborg Palace, you can easily walk from the heart of Copenhagen. It's a short stroll from other central attractions like Nyhavn or the Marble Church. If you're taking public transportation, the nearest metro station is Kongens Nytorv, which is about a ten-minute walk away. Several bus lines also pass nearby, making it quite accessible from various parts of the city.

Visiting Amalienborg Palace is a unique experience, though it is important to note that the palace itself is not open to the public. The primary attraction is the daily changing of the guard, which takes place at noon. This ceremony is a spectacle of precision and tradition, and it's free to watch. The guards, in their distinctive uniforms and tall bearskin hats, perform a formal procession and change guard in a manner that reflects centuries of royal tradition.

While the interior of the palace is off-limits to visitors, the Amalienborg Museum, located in one of the palaces, offers a fascinating glimpse into the royal family's life. The museum is situated at the address of the palace complex, and entry typically costs around 120 DKK for adults, with reduced rates for children, students, and seniors. It's worth checking the official website for the latest information on ticket prices and opening hours. The museum showcases royal artifacts, portraits, and rooms that offer insight into the daily life of the Danish monarchy.

For the best experience, I recommend arriving a bit early to secure a good viewing spot for the changing of the guard ceremony. The palace square gets crowded, especially in peak tourist seasons, so finding a spot along the railing will give you a clear view of the action. If you're interested in learning more about the history and significance of the ceremony, consider joining a guided walking tour that includes Amalienborg Palace as part of its itinerary.

The square itself is an elegant setting, with the four palaces, the Frederik's Church in the background, and the equestrian statue of King Frederik V in the center. It's an ideal spot for taking photographs and soaking in the royal ambiance. The open space around the square provides a grand perspective of the palace's architecture and the ceremonial routines.

If you have time after visiting Amalienborg Palace, you can explore the surrounding area. The nearby Frederiksstaden district offers charming streets and scenic waterfront views. You might also visit the Marble Church (Frederiks Kirke), which is just a short walk away and boasts a stunning dome and intricate interiors.

Overall, Amalienborg Palace, even though its interiors are not open to the public, offers a rich experience through its historical significance, the impressive changing of the guard ceremony, and the insights provided by the Amalienborg

Museum. It's a cornerstone of Copenhagen's royal heritage and a must-visit for anyone interested in the grandeur of Danish royalty.

The Round Tower: A Panoramic View of the City

The Round Tower, known as Rundetårn in Danish, is a charming historical landmark located at Købmagergade 52A, 1150 Copenhagen K. As I arrived at this iconic structure, I was immediately struck by its unique design and the sense of history that seemed to envelop the space. The Round Tower was built in the early 17th century by King Christian IV and is notable for its circular design and the impressive view it offers of Copenhagen.

Getting to the Round Tower is straightforward. It is centrally located and easily accessible from various parts of the city. If you're coming by public transportation, you can take the metro to the Nørreport Station, which is a short walk away. Alternatively, if you're staying in the city center, the tower is within walking distance from popular areas like Strøget, the main shopping street, and the historic Nyhavn waterfront. You'll find it nestled amidst the bustling Købmagergade, so keep an eye out for its distinctive round shape.

Entrance to the Round Tower costs about 40 DKK for adults, with reduced rates for children, students, and seniors. The ticket gives you access to the main attraction: the spiral ramp that leads to the observation deck. This ramp is a fascinating architectural feature, gently winding its way up to the top without stairs, which is a testament to the innovative design of the era. It's both a physical journey and a glimpse into historical architectural ingenuity.

As you ascend the ramp, you'll pass through various historical exhibitions and displays. The interior of the tower has been thoughtfully curated to showcase aspects of Danish history and astronomy, reflecting its past use as an astronomical observatory. The exhibits provide a great context for the views you'll enjoy from the top.

Once you reach the observation deck, the panoramic view of Copenhagen is nothing short of breathtaking. From this vantage point, you can see the city's charming rooftops, the spires of its many churches, and even distant landmarks such as the Little Mermaid statue and the waterfront. The deck provides a perfect spot for photographs and to simply take in the city's scenic beauty.

If you have time, I recommend visiting the tower in the late afternoon or early evening to enjoy the golden hues of sunset over Copenhagen. The light at this time can add a magical quality to the cityscape. Additionally, the Round Tower often hosts various cultural events and exhibitions, so checking their schedule beforehand might provide an opportunity to experience something special during your visit.

The surrounding area is also worth exploring. After your visit, you might stroll down Købmagergade, which is lined with shops and cafes where you can relax and soak in the lively atmosphere. Nearby, you can find the historic University of Copenhagen and the charming old streets of the Latin Quarter, adding to the overall charm of your visit to the Round Tower.

In summary, the Round Tower offers a unique combination of historical interest and panoramic views. It's a must-visit for anyone wanting to experience Copenhagen from a new perspective while enjoying a piece of the city's rich history. The gentle climb up the spiral ramp, the historical insights, and the spectacular view make for a memorable visit that captures the essence of Copenhagen's architectural and cultural heritage.

Christiansborg Palace: The Seat of Danish Parliament

Christiansborg Palace, located at Prins Jørgens Gård 1, 1218 Copenhagen K, stands as a grand symbol of Denmark's political history and architectural prowess. My visit to this impressive palace was an enlightening experience, immersing me in the rich heritage of Danish governance and regal splendor.

To reach Christiansborg Palace, I found it convenient to use the Copenhagen Metro. The nearest station is Kongens Nytorv, from which the palace is just a short walk. Alternatively, if you're staying in the city center, you can easily reach it by foot. The palace is centrally located on Slotsholmen, an island in the heart of Copenhagen, surrounded by picturesque waterways and historical buildings.

The entrance to Christiansborg Palace is generally priced at around 160 DKK for adults, with discounts available for children, students, and seniors. The ticket grants access to several parts of the palace, including the royal reception rooms, the parliamentary chambers, and the old ruins of the original palace. It's worth noting that the palace is still an active government building, so certain areas may be restricted based on parliamentary activities and events.

As I walked through the majestic halls of Christiansborg, I was struck by the grandeur of the royal reception rooms. These rooms, with their opulent furnishings and historical artworks, provide a fascinating glimpse into the life of Danish royalty. The Great Hall, with its splendid tapestries and grand chandeliers, is particularly impressive and showcases the rich artistic heritage of Denmark.

One of the highlights of the visit was exploring the Danish Parliament chambers. Christiansborg Palace serves as the seat of the Danish Parliament, so visitors get a unique chance to see the chambers where the country's important political decisions are made. The rooms are elegantly designed and provide a deep insight into Denmark's democratic process.

The palace also houses the Supreme Court and the Prime Minister's Office, which are not accessible to the public but add to the building's significance as a center of Danish governance. A special treat is the view from the palace tower. For a small additional fee, you can take an elevator ride up to the tower, which offers panoramic views of Copenhagen and its surrounding areas. This viewpoint provides a fantastic opportunity for photography and to appreciate the city's layout from above.

For a more historical experience, I wandered through the ruins of the original Christiansborg Palace located in the basement. These ancient ruins date back to the early medieval period and offer a fascinating contrast to the grandeur of the current palace structure.

If you're planning a visit, consider timing your trip to coincide with one of the palace's guided tours. These tours provide in-depth information about the history and architecture of Christiansborg and are led by knowledgeable guides who can offer additional context and answer any questions.

After exploring the palace, I enjoyed a leisurely stroll around Slotsholmen. The island is home to other notable sites, including the Copenhagen City Hall and the charming Nyhavn waterfront, making it easy to combine your visit to Christiansborg with a broader exploration of Copenhagen's historical heart.

Christiansborg Palace offers a compelling mix of royal history, political significance, and architectural beauty. From the opulent reception rooms to the impressive parliament chambers and the ancient ruins, there's plenty to discover. Whether you're interested in Danish history, politics, or simply enjoying the grandeur of a royal palace, Christiansborg is a must-visit destination that provides a deep and enriching experience of Copenhagen's cultural and historical heritage.

CHAPTER 6.
MUSEUMS AND ART GALLERIES

The National Museum of Denmark

The National Museum of Denmark, located at Ny Vestergade 10, 1471 Copenhagen K, is a treasure trove of Danish history and culture. My visit there was a journey through time, offering a captivating look at Denmark's past and its place in the wider world.

To get to the National Museum, I used the Copenhagen Metro. The nearest station is Rådhuspladsen, which is a short walk away from the museum. If you prefer walking, it's an easy stroll through the city center, making it a convenient spot to visit while exploring other nearby attractions.

The museum's entrance fee is around 95 DKK for adults, with discounts for students, seniors, and children. The price is well worth it for the extensive collection and engaging exhibits you'll find inside. The museum is housed in a grand 19th-century building, and even before stepping inside, you're greeted by its impressive architecture.

Once inside, I was struck by the sheer variety of exhibits. The National Museum is divided into several sections, each showcasing different aspects of Danish history and culture. One of my favorite parts was the Danish Prehistory exhibit, which features artifacts from the Stone Age, Bronze Age, and Viking Age. The well-preserved Viking weapons, jewelry, and runestones were fascinating and provided a vivid glimpse into Denmark's early history.

The museum also has a rich collection of ethnographic artifacts from around the world. Walking through these exhibits, I was able to see how Denmark's colonial past has influenced its cultural exchanges with other nations. The artifacts from Greenland, the Faroe Islands, and other territories were particularly interesting, offering insights into the diverse cultures that have interacted with Denmark over the centuries.

Another highlight was the Royal Collection, which displays items from Denmark's royal families, including royal regalia, ceremonial objects, and portraits. Seeing these items up close allowed me to appreciate the opulence and history of Denmark's monarchy.

The museum is well-organized, making it easy to navigate through its various exhibits. For those who want to delve deeper, the museum offers guided tours and audio guides that provide additional context and stories behind the artifacts. I found the audio guide particularly helpful in understanding the significance of the exhibits and the historical context.

To make the most of your visit, I recommend setting aside at least a few hours to explore the museum. There's a lot to see, and taking your time will allow you to fully appreciate the exhibits. If you're interested in learning more about specific topics, check the museum's schedule for any special exhibitions or events that might be taking place during your visit.

After exploring the museum, you can relax in the museum café, which offers a selection of snacks and beverages. It's a pleasant spot to unwind and reflect on what you've seen. Additionally, there's a museum shop where you can purchase souvenirs, books, and replicas of some of the museum's artifacts.

The National Museum of Denmark is a must-visit for anyone interested in Danish history and culture. Its diverse collection, engaging exhibits, and beautiful setting make it a rewarding experience. Whether you're a history buff or just curious about Denmark's past, the museum offers a comprehensive and enjoyable journey through time.

The Danish National Gallery (SMK)

The Danish National Gallery, known locally as Statens Museum for Kunst (SMK), is a must-visit for anyone interested in art. Located at Sølvgade 48-50, 1307 Copenhagen K, the gallery is conveniently situated in the heart of the city, making it easy to include in your sightseeing plans.

To get to the gallery, I found that taking the Copenhagen Metro is the simplest way. The nearest station is Nørreport, which is just a short walk away from the gallery. Alternatively, if you prefer walking, it's a pleasant stroll through some of Copenhagen's charming streets, with plenty of cafes and shops to explore along the way.

When I arrived at SMK, the grand entrance set the tone for what was to come. The gallery's collection spans from the Middle Ages to contemporary art, showcasing a rich tapestry of Danish and international artworks. The entrance fee is around 130 DKK for adults, with various discounts for students, seniors, and children, making it accessible for everyone.

The gallery's collection is extensive and well-organized. I started with the Danish Golden Age paintings, which feature works by artists like Christen Købke and C.W. Eckersberg. These paintings offer a glimpse into Denmark's 19th-century society and landscapes, and their detailed craftsmanship was truly impressive.

Next, I explored the modern and contemporary sections. The gallery houses works by notable Danish artists such as Asger Jorn and Per Kirkeby, as well as international figures like Picasso and Matisse. The modern art collection is vibrant and thought-provoking, with pieces that range from abstract to conceptual art.

One of the highlights of my visit was the gallery's special exhibitions. SMK regularly hosts temporary exhibitions that delve into specific themes or showcase the work of particular artists. Checking the gallery's website in advance can help you find out what exhibitions will be on during your visit. I found these exhibitions to be incredibly engaging, offering fresh perspectives and insights into various art movements and trends.

The gallery is spacious, with several floors to explore. The layout makes it easy to navigate through different periods and styles of art. I also appreciated the informative plaques and digital guides available throughout the gallery, which provided context and background for the artworks.

After wandering through the galleries, I enjoyed a break at the museum café, located within the gallery. It offers a selection of pastries, sandwiches, and coffee, which was a perfect way to recharge. The café also has a lovely outdoor seating area where you can relax and enjoy views of the surrounding park.

The museum shop is another great spot to visit. It features a range of art-related items, from postcards and prints to art books and unique gifts. I found it a nice place to pick up a souvenir or two.

The Danish National Gallery is a fantastic destination for art lovers and anyone looking to immerse themselves in Danish culture. Its extensive collection, engaging exhibitions, and beautiful setting make it a worthwhile visit. Whether you're an art enthusiast or just curious about Denmark's artistic heritage, SMK offers a rewarding and enjoyable experience.

The Ny Carlsberg Glyptotek

Visiting the Ny Carlsberg Glyptotek was one of the highlights of my time in Copenhagen. This museum, located at Dantes Plads 7, 1556 Copenhagen K, is an exceptional place for anyone interested in art and history.

Getting to the Ny Carlsberg Glyptotek is straightforward. I took the Copenhagen Metro to the Rådhuspladsen station, which is conveniently close to the museum. From there, it's just a short walk, and I found the way well-signposted. If you prefer, you can also hop on a bus or even enjoy a leisurely stroll from other central locations in the city.

Upon arriving, the Glyptotek's grand entrance gave a strong first impression. The museum itself is housed in a beautiful building that combines classical architecture with modern touches, making it a sight to behold. The entrance fee is around 115 DKK for adults, with various discounts available for students, seniors, and children. It's worth noting that the museum often offers free admission on certain days or times, so it's a good idea to check their website before you go.

The Ny Carlsberg Glyptotek is renowned for its impressive collection of sculptures and ancient artifacts. The museum's collection is split between two main sections: ancient Mediterranean art and 19th-century French art. I started with the ancient section, which features a stunning array of sculptures from ancient Egypt, Greece, and Rome. The collection includes everything from intricately carved statues to delicate reliefs, each piece offering a glimpse into the artistic achievements of ancient civilizations.

One of my favorite parts was the museum's collection of Roman sculptures. These works are displayed in the beautiful winter garden, which is a lovely, light-filled space filled with lush plants and a tranquil atmosphere. It provided a peaceful contrast to the impressive but sometimes overwhelming scale of the artworks.

Moving on to the 19th-century French art collection, I was captivated by the works of artists like Claude Monet, Edgar Degas, and Pierre-Auguste Renoir. The museum has a fantastic assortment of impressionist and post-impressionist paintings, which are displayed in elegantly designed galleries. The way the artworks are presented allows for an immersive experience, where you can really appreciate the details and techniques used by these renowned artists.

The Glyptotek also offers rotating exhibitions, which feature a range of themes and artists. During my visit, there was a special exhibition on Danish Golden Age painting, which was a fantastic opportunity to explore more of Denmark's rich artistic heritage.

The museum's café is another great place to relax. Situated in a charming room with views of the winter garden, it serves a variety of light meals and refreshments. I enjoyed a coffee and a pastry here, which was a pleasant way to unwind after exploring the galleries.

Before leaving, I made sure to stop by the museum shop, which has a selection of art books, souvenirs, and replicas of some of the museum's most famous pieces. It's a good spot to pick up a unique gift or memento from your visit.

The Ny Carlsberg Glyptotek is a fantastic destination for art lovers and anyone interested in exploring ancient and modern art. Its beautiful setting, rich collections, and engaging exhibitions make it a must-visit. Whether you're an art enthusiast or just looking to enjoy a day out in Copenhagen, the Glyptotek offers a memorable and enriching experience.

The Louisiana Museum of Modern Art

Visiting the Louisiana Museum of Modern Art was a remarkable experience that I'll always treasure. Located at Gl. Strandvej 13, 3050 Humlebæk, Denmark, the museum is set in a picturesque location right by the Øresund Strait, offering stunning views of the water and surrounding landscape.

Getting to the Louisiana Museum is quite convenient. I took a train from Copenhagen's central station to Humlebæk Station, which is a relaxing journey of about 35 minutes. From Humlebæk Station, it's just a short walk to the museum. There are clear signs directing you to Louisiana, and the walk through the charming village is pleasant. Alternatively, you can also take a bus or drive if you prefer, and there's ample parking available.

As for the entrance, the museum charges an admission fee of around 145 DKK for adults. There are reduced rates for students, seniors, and children, and sometimes the museum offers free admission on specific days, so it's worth checking their website before planning your visit.

The Louisiana Museum of Modern Art is renowned for its impressive collection of contemporary art and its beautiful setting. Upon entering, I was immediately struck by the museum's blend of modern architecture and natural surroundings. The museum's design seamlessly integrates with the landscape, providing a unique viewing experience. The open, airy spaces and large windows frame the stunning views of the gardens and the sea, making the art feel part of a larger, harmonious environment.

The museum's collection spans from the late 20th century to the present day, featuring works by both Danish and international artists. I was particularly impressed by the variety and depth of the exhibits. The permanent collection includes pieces from iconic artists such as Picasso, Warhol, and Giacometti. The museum also hosts temporary exhibitions, which cover a wide range of themes and mediums. During my visit, there was a fascinating exhibition on contemporary sculpture, which included some interactive and multimedia installations that were engaging and thought-provoking.

One of the highlights of my visit was exploring the museum's sculpture park. The outdoor area is beautifully landscaped and features works by artists like Alexander Calder and Henry Moore. Walking through the park, I enjoyed the interplay between the sculptures and the natural environment. It's a serene spot to take a break and appreciate art in a more relaxed setting.

Inside, the Louisiana offers several galleries, each with its own theme and atmosphere. The museum's layout is designed to encourage exploration and discovery. The art is displayed in a way that invites you to linger and reflect, and the space itself is as much a part of the experience as the artworks. The museum's café, located with views over the garden and the sea, is a perfect place to take a break. I had a chance to enjoy a light lunch there, with fresh, local ingredients and a selection of Danish pastries.

Before leaving, I visited the museum shop, which has a great selection of art books, prints, and unique gifts. It's a good place to pick up something to remember your visit by or to find a special present for someone back home.

Overall, the Louisiana Museum of Modern Art is a must-visit for anyone interested in contemporary art and beautiful surroundings. Its combination of striking architecture, impressive collections, and stunning location makes it a standout destination. Whether you're an art aficionado or just looking for a relaxing day out, Louisiana offers a rich and enjoyable experience.

Designmuseum Danmark

Designmuseum Denmark, located at Bredgade 68, 1260 Copenhagen K, Denmark, offers a captivating journey into the world of design. My visit there was a fascinating exploration of Danish and international design, showcasing everything from historic pieces to contemporary innovations.

To get to the Designmuseum, I took the bus from Copenhagen Central Station, which was a straightforward and quick ride. The museum is well-situated in the heart of Copenhagen, so it's also easy to reach on foot from many central locations. If you prefer the train, you can take a short walk from the nearest metro station at Kongens Nytorv. For those driving, there is limited street parking nearby, but public transport is a convenient option.

The museum charges an entrance fee of about 130 DKK for adults, with reduced rates for students, seniors, and children. It's worth checking their website for any special offers or free admission days before you go. When I visited, there was a temporary exhibition on Danish design icons, which was included in the standard ticket price.

Designmuseum Denmark is housed in a beautiful historic building, which adds a layer of charm to the experience. The museum's exhibitions span a broad range of design disciplines, from furniture and textiles to industrial design and graphic arts. As I wandered through the galleries, I was struck by the meticulous presentation of each exhibit. The museum's layout is thoughtfully designed, allowing visitors to appreciate the nuances of each piece while providing ample context about the designers and their work.

One of the highlights of my visit was the collection of Danish furniture design, featuring iconic pieces by designers such as Arne Jacobsen and Hans Wegner. The museum's exhibits not only display these masterpieces but also offer insights into the design process and the cultural impact of the pieces. I spent a lot of time exploring the interactive displays, which provided a deeper understanding of the design principles and craftsmanship behind the works.

The museum also has a section dedicated to contemporary design, which includes innovative projects and sustainable design solutions. This part of the museum was particularly engaging, showcasing how modern designers are addressing current challenges through creativity and technology.

The museum's café, located within the premises, offers a pleasant space to relax and enjoy a coffee or light snack. The café's design complements the museum's aesthetic, making it a perfect spot to unwind after exploring the exhibits. I had a chance to enjoy a delicious Danish pastry while soaking in the creative atmosphere of the café.

Before leaving, I visited the museum shop, which features a curated selection of design-related items. From stylish homewares to unique souvenirs, the shop offers something for every design enthusiast. I found a beautiful piece of Danish ceramics that made for a perfect memento of my visit.

Overall, Designmuseum Denmark is a must-visit for anyone interested in design and its evolution. The combination of a rich collection, engaging exhibitions, and a charming setting makes it a standout destination in Copenhagen. Whether you're a design aficionado or just curious about the creative world, the museum provides an enriching experience that's both educational and inspiring.

The David Collection

The David Collection, located at 30 Kronprinsessegade, 1306 Copenhagen K, Denmark, is a gem of a museum that offers a deep dive into Islamic art and culture, along with an impressive collection of European art. My visit to the David Collection was a unique and enriching experience, revealing an exquisite array of artifacts and artworks.

Reaching the museum was quite straightforward. I took a short walk from the nearby Nørreport Station, which is well-connected by metro and trains. For those arriving by bus, several routes stop close to the museum. If you prefer to drive, there's street parking available, although it can be limited in this busy area of Copenhagen.

The David Collection has an entrance fee of around 120 DKK for adults, though it's free on Tuesday afternoons, which is a fantastic way to save if your schedule allows. The museum's website is a good resource for checking current ticket prices and any special exhibitions that might be on during your visit.

The museum is housed in a beautiful 19th-century building that complements the elegance of its collections. As I entered, I was struck by the serene and sophisticated ambiance, which sets the tone for exploring its diverse exhibits. The collection is divided into several thematic sections, each showcasing different aspects of art and history.

One of the highlights of the David Collection is its extensive Islamic art collection, which spans several centuries and regions. As I wandered through this section, I was mesmerized by the intricate patterns, calligraphy, and craftsmanship on display. The collection includes everything from beautifully decorated ceramics to finely detailed textiles and manuscripts. The museum does an excellent job of providing context and background for each piece, which enhanced my understanding and appreciation of the art.

The European collection at the David Collection is equally impressive, featuring a selection of paintings, sculptures, and decorative arts from the 18th and 19th centuries. I was particularly fascinated by the pieces from the Rococo period, which were displayed with a sense of grandeur and detail that brought the era to life. The museum's thoughtful curation allowed me to explore the connections between different artistic traditions and styles.

The museum's layout is very visitor-friendly, with clear signage and informative plaques next to each exhibit. I appreciated the way the exhibits are organized, making it easy to follow the different themes and periods. The atmosphere was quiet and contemplative, perfect for absorbing the rich content of the collections.

Before leaving, I visited the museum shop, which offers a selection of art books, prints, and unique souvenirs related to the museum's collections. I found a beautiful art book that captured some of the highlights of the Islamic art collection, which made a perfect keepsake from my visit.

Overall, the David Collection offers a fascinating and well-rounded museum experience. Its diverse range of artworks, combined with the elegant setting, creates a memorable visit for anyone interested in art and history. Whether you're a seasoned art lover or just looking to explore something new in Copenhagen, the David Collection is a must-see destination that provides a rich and rewarding experience.

CHAPTER 7.
CULINARY SCENE

Traditional Danish Cuisine: Smørrebrød, Frikadeller, and More

Exploring traditional Danish cuisine was one of the highlights of my trip to Copenhagen. The city is rich with culinary traditions that reflect its history and culture, and trying the local dishes was an experience that truly immersed me in Danish life. Here's a detailed look at some of the classic Danish foods I encountered, along with a few health tips for those with dietary restrictions.

One of the first dishes I tried was smørrebrød, a quintessential Danish open-faced sandwich. The moment I tasted it, I understood why it's such a beloved part of Danish culture. Typically served on dense rye bread, smørrebrød is topped with a variety of ingredients, ranging from pickled herring to roast beef. My first smørrebrød featured pickled herring with onions and capers, which was a delightful mix of tangy, sweet, and salty flavors. The texture of the herring, combined with the crunch of the rye bread and the fresh bite of the onions, made for a truly satisfying meal. The Danish take their smørrebrød seriously, and each variation I tried was carefully crafted with an eye for both taste and presentation.

Next on my list was frikadeller, Danish meatballs that are a staple in any Danish kitchen. I remember my first bite of these juicy meatballs vividly. They were seasoned with a blend of spices and herbs, and the texture was perfectly tender, not too dense. Served with a side of creamy potatoes and rich gravy, frikadeller offered a comforting, hearty meal. I found that frikadeller were often enjoyed with a side of pickled vegetables, which added a nice contrast to the richness of the meatballs.

Another traditional dish that I enjoyed was rødgrød med fløde, a quintessential Danish dessert made from red berries and served with cream. The first spoonful of this sweet and slightly tart dessert was a revelation. The berries, which were often a mix of strawberries, raspberries, and currants, created a vibrant and refreshing flavor, and the cream added a rich, velvety finish. It's a simple yet elegant dessert that perfectly captures the essence of Danish summer flavors.

I also tried roast pork, known in Denmark as stegt flæsk, which is often served with parsley sauce and potatoes. This dish was a real treat, with crispy, savory pork belly complemented by a creamy, herb-infused sauce. The combination of the crispy skin and tender meat was absolutely delicious, and the whole meal was wonderfully satisfying.

Lastly, I experienced the traditional Danish rye bread, or rugbrød, which is used as a base for many Danish sandwiches. This dense, dark bread is packed with grains and seeds, and it has a slightly nutty flavor. Eating it with various toppings like cheese or cold cuts provided a hearty and nutritious start to my day.

For those with allergies or dietary restrictions, Danish cuisine can present some challenges, but there are ways to enjoy the traditional flavors while staying within dietary limits. Many Danish dishes contain gluten, so if you have a gluten intolerance, look for options that are naturally gluten-free or inquire about gluten-free alternatives. For dairy allergies, consider asking for dairy-free substitutes where possible, as some dishes, particularly desserts, may include cream or milk. Vegetarians might find it a bit more challenging, as traditional Danish cuisine often features meat and fish, but many restaurants in Copenhagen offer vegetarian versions of popular dishes or have separate vegetarian menus.

In summary, trying traditional Danish cuisine was a deeply satisfying experience. From the open-faced sandwiches of smørrebrød to the hearty frikadeller and the refreshing rødgrød med fløde, each dish told a story of Danish culture and culinary tradition. With a little planning, those with dietary restrictions can also enjoy the flavors of Denmark, ensuring that everyone can have a taste of this wonderful cuisine.

Copenhagen's Michelin-Starred Restaurants

Copenhagen offers a rich and varied dining and nightlife scene, reflecting its status as a vibrant, cosmopolitan city. Whether you're in the mood for fine dining, casual eateries, or lively nightlife, Copenhagen has something to cater to every taste.

Must-Try Local Eateries
For a true taste of Copenhagen, start with Noma, located at Refshalevej 96. Renowned globally, this restaurant offers an upscale dining experience with a focus on New Nordic cuisine. The atmosphere here is chic and innovative, with a minimalistic design that lets the food take center stage. Expect to pay around 1,500 to 2,500 DKK per person for a tasting menu that showcases local ingredients in extraordinary ways.

Another exceptional spot is Geranium, at Per Henrik Lunds Vej 2. This three-Michelin-starred restaurant provides a unique dining experience with a sophisticated atmosphere. The price range is similarly high-end, with tasting menus costing around 2,000 to 3,000 DKK. The signature dishes here are artfully presented, featuring seasonal ingredients that highlight Denmark's natural bounty.

For a more laid-back, yet equally delightful experience, head to Torvehallerne, located at Frederiksberg Allé 48. This bustling food market offers a range of local delights from different vendors. You can sample everything from smørrebrød, traditional Danish open-faced sandwiches, to fresh seafood and artisanal pastries. Prices here are much more accessible, with snacks and meals ranging from 50 to 200 DKK.

Nightlife Scene
When the sun sets, Copenhagen comes alive with a diverse array of nightlife options. For a relaxed atmosphere with a great selection of craft cocktails, try The Jane at Gråbrødretorv 8. The ambiance is sophisticated yet casual, making it a perfect spot for a night out with friends or a romantic evening. The cocktails here are creatively crafted, with an emphasis on quality ingredients.

If you're into live music, head to Vega at Vesterbro, located at Vesterbro 15. This iconic venue hosts a range of performances from international bands to local artists, covering genres from rock to electronic. The schedule is packed with events throughout the week, so you're likely to find something that suits your musical tastes.

For dancing and high-energy nightlife, check out Culture Box at Kronprinsensgade 54. Known for its vibrant electronic music scene, this nightclub attracts top DJs and offers a high-energy atmosphere. Expect to find a mix of techno, house, and other electronic genres. The club is a favorite among locals and tourists alike for its dynamic vibe and impressive sound system.

Cultural and Local Insights
Dining in Copenhagen often includes a focus on seasonal and local ingredients, reflecting Denmark's commitment to sustainability. When dining out, it's common for restaurants

to embrace a casual yet refined approach, with many places offering a relaxed dress code.

In terms of nightlife, Copenhagen has a friendly and open atmosphere, with a strong emphasis on enjoying oneself in a respectful manner. Pubs and bars often have an early closing time compared to some other major cities, so be sure to start your evening early if you want to make the most of it.

Hidden Gems
For a unique experience, visit Mikkeller Bar at Viktoriagade 8. This hidden gem offers a wide selection of craft beers brewed by the renowned Mikkeller brewery. The atmosphere is laid-back, with a focus on quality brews and a knowledgeable staff ready to help you choose the perfect drink.

Another lesser-known spot is Kødbyens Fiskebar, located at Fiskebaren 7. This seafood restaurant in the trendy Meatpacking District combines a casual vibe with excellent food. The fresh seafood, including oysters and fish dishes, is a standout here, and the unpretentious setting makes it a local favorite.

Safety and Practical Tips
When exploring Copenhagen's nightlife, it's important to use reliable transportation options such as taxis or public transit. The city's public transport system is efficient and safe, with buses and trains operating until late at night. Always keep an eye on your belongings, as with any major city, and be aware of your surroundings.

Copenhagen has strict regulations regarding alcohol consumption, especially in public areas. Be sure to enjoy your drinks responsibly and respect local customs and laws.

Copenhagen's dining and nightlife scene is as diverse as the city itself, offering everything from high-end restaurants and bustling food markets to lively bars and unique clubs. Whether you're savoring a tasting menu at a world-class restaurant, enjoying a craft cocktail, or dancing the night away, Copenhagen provides a rich tapestry of experiences that will make your visit memorable. Embrace the city's vibrant culinary and entertainment offerings, and you'll find plenty to explore and enjoy.

Street Food: The Best Markets and Food Halls

Copenhagen's street food scene is a delightful blend of flavors and cultures, offering a casual yet vibrant dining experience. The city's markets and food halls provide a fantastic opportunity to sample a variety of delicious dishes while soaking up the lively atmosphere.

Torvehallerne is one of Copenhagen's most popular food markets, located at Frederiksberg Allé 48. This bustling market features over 60 stalls, each offering a different culinary delight. From fresh seafood and artisan cheeses to gourmet sandwiches and pastries, there's something to suit every taste. I was particularly impressed by the selection of smørrebrød, traditional Danish open-faced sandwiches, which were both flavorful and beautifully presented. The market has a relaxed vibe, making it a great spot for a leisurely lunch or snack. Prices are reasonable, with many items ranging from 50 to 150 DKK.

Another fantastic spot is Reffen, located at Refshalevej 167. This street food market is set in a vibrant industrial area and offers a diverse range of international cuisines. Here, you can enjoy everything from Korean BBQ and Mexican tacos to vegan burgers and freshly made falafel. The atmosphere at Reffen is lively and casual, with plenty of outdoor seating that's perfect for enjoying the summer weather. I particularly enjoyed the street food stalls that offered unique fusion dishes and creative presentations. Prices at Reffen are also quite affordable, with most dishes costing between 70 and 150 DKK.

For a unique experience, visit the Copenhagen Street Food Market at Papirøen, situated on an old paper mill island at Trangravsvej 14. Although the location has moved since my visit, the spirit of the market remains vibrant. The market featured a rotating selection of food trucks and stalls serving everything from gourmet burgers to exotic Middle Eastern dishes. The setting was relaxed and informal, with communal seating that encouraged mingling with fellow food lovers. The prices were similar to other markets, with most meals priced around 80 to 120 DKK.

These street food markets and food halls are great places to experience Copenhagen's diverse culinary scene in a casual setting. Each offers a unique atmosphere and a wide range of options, making it easy to find something that appeals to your taste. Whether you're grabbing a quick bite or enjoying a leisurely meal, these markets provide a wonderful glimpse into the city's food culture.

Cafés and Bakeries: Hygge and Danish Pastries

Copenhagen is renowned for its cozy cafés and delightful bakeries, where you can experience the essence of Danish "hygge" – that warm, inviting feeling of comfort and contentment. The city's café culture is rich, with numerous spots offering delicious pastries, aromatic coffee, and a welcoming atmosphere.

One must-visit café is The Laundromat Café, located at Elmegade 15. This charming spot combines the casual vibe of a laundromat with a cozy café atmosphere. It's perfect for a relaxed coffee break or a leisurely breakfast. The café serves a variety of delicious pastries, including Danish cinnamon rolls and buttery croissants. Their coffee is consistently good, and the ambiance is very laid-back. I enjoyed their Danish pastry selection, which was fresh and perfectly sweet. Prices are reasonable, with pastries generally costing around 30 to 50 DKK and coffee between 30 and 50 DKK.

Another favorite is Café Norden, situated at Østergade 10. This café is known for its elegant interior and extensive menu. It's a great spot for both breakfast and lunch, offering everything from classic Danish open-faced sandwiches to hearty soups. Their bakery selection includes classic Danish pastries like wienerbrød, which are flaky and filled with rich, sweet fillings. The ambiance is both stylish and comfortable, making it an excellent place for a leisurely coffee or a light meal. Prices here range from 50 to 100 DKK for pastries and 80 to 150 DKK for main dishes.

For a true taste of Danish pastries, visit Bageri K, located at Tullinsgade 1. This bakery is a local favorite, known for its high-quality pastries and traditional baking techniques. They offer a range of delectable options, from buttery croissants to decadent Danish butter cookies. The bakery has a welcoming atmosphere, with a display case full of beautifully crafted pastries that are hard to resist. Prices are very reasonable, with most pastries priced around 25 to 40 DKK.

These cafés and bakeries embody the Danish spirit of hygge and are perfect spots to unwind while enjoying some of the best pastries the city has to offer. Whether you're stopping by for a quick coffee or settling in for a leisurely breakfast, you'll find that Copenhagen's café culture is both charming and satisfying.

The Craft Beer Scene: Breweries and Beer Bars

Copenhagen's craft beer scene is a vibrant and exciting part of the city's culture, offering a range of breweries and beer bars where you can sample unique and flavorful brews. The city's craft beer movement is thriving, with numerous spots showcasing both local and international beers.

One of the standout places is To Øl Bar, located at Vesterbro 4. This bar is known for its innovative approach to brewing and offers a diverse selection of craft beers. The atmosphere is casual and relaxed, making it a great spot to enjoy a drink with friends. They have a rotating selection of their own beers and other craft brews from around the world. Prices for a pint typically range from 50 to 80 DKK, and the staff are knowledgeable and happy to help you find something you'll enjoy.

Another excellent spot is Mikkeller Bar, which can be found at Viktoriagade 8. Mikkeller is a well-known name in the craft beer world, and their bar in Copenhagen lives up to its reputation. The place has a cozy, yet modern feel, with a wide range of Mikkeller's own brews alongside guest beers from various breweries. You can try their distinctive and often experimental beers, which are both intriguing and delicious. Expect to pay around 60 to 90 DKK for a glass of their beer.

For a more traditional brewery experience, visit Nørrebro Bryghus, located at Ryesgade 3. This brewery combines a friendly atmosphere with a robust selection of house-brewed beers. The space is inviting, with a focus on both brewing and enjoying craft beer. They offer guided tours and tastings, which are a great way to learn more about the brewing process and sample a variety of beers. A pint here typically costs between 50 and 70 DKK.

Exploring Copenhagen's craft beer scene is a rewarding experience, with many options to suit different tastes and preferences. From innovative new brews to classic styles, the city's breweries and beer bars offer something for everyone. Whether you're a craft beer aficionado or just looking to try something new, Copenhagen has a wealth of options to discover and enjoy.

Festivals and Traditions:

Experiencing Danish Culture
A Danish Adventure: From Maypoles to Mermaid Parades
I've always been curious about Danish culture, so when I had the chance to visit Copenhagen in the summer, I was excited. I didn't expect to dive into such lively festivals and traditions that would make me laugh, feel surprised, and completely enchanted.

The first festival I experienced was the Maypole celebration. Imagine a huge, colorful pole decorated with ribbons, surrounded by people dancing and singing traditional songs. It felt like stepping into a fairytale. I joined in, spinning and jumping around with everyone.

While dancing, I met a local named Lars. He said, "This is the best day of the year! We dance, sing, and celebrate spring. It's a tradition that has been around for hundreds of years."

I asked Lars about other festivals I should see. "There are many," he said. "You should go to the Mermaid Parade. It's a bit crazy but really fun."

So, I went to the Mermaid Parade. Imagine hundreds of people dressed as mermaids, sea creatures, and other ocean beings, parading through the streets of Copenhagen. There were mermaids on bikes, mermen drumming, and even a giant inflatable octopus. It was the most unusual and amazing thing I had ever seen.

Watching the parade, I couldn't stop laughing. The Danes are great at making traditions unique and memorable. They know how to have fun and aren't afraid to be a bit silly.

My time in Copenhagen was full of other cultural experiences, like watching traditional dances and tasting delicious Danish pastries. But the festivals and traditions were what made the trip unforgettable. They showed me the heart of Danish culture, and I left feeling inspired and entertained.

If you're looking for a place with a mix of history, culture, and fun, I strongly recommend visiting Copenhagen. Be ready for surprises and join in the celebrations. You might find yourself dancing around a maypole or joining a mermaid parade. It's an experience you'll never forget.

CHAPTER 8.
DAY TRIPS FROM COPENHAGEN

Kronborg Castle: The Home of Hamlet

Kronborg Castle, located in Helsingør, just north of Copenhagen, is a must-visit for anyone interested in history and literature. This magnificent castle, perched on a cliff overlooking the Øresund Strait, is best known as the setting for Shakespeare's famous play, "Hamlet."

When you arrive at Kronborg Castle, you'll be struck by its impressive size and architectural beauty. The castle is a mix of Renaissance and medieval styles, with its grand towers and detailed brickwork making it a true landmark. As you walk through its gates, you'll feel like you've stepped back in time.

Inside the castle, you can explore a variety of rooms, including the grand ballroom, where elaborate events were once held. The castle's hallways are filled with historical artifacts, and the old chambers give you a glimpse into the royal life of the past. Don't miss the chance to see the King's Chamber and the Queen's Chamber, where you can imagine the opulent life of Danish royalty.

One of the highlights of the castle is the castle's theater, which still hosts performances today. This adds to the historical charm and makes you feel connected to the past, as if you were experiencing the same dramatic moments that Shakespeare imagined.

To get to Kronborg Castle from Copenhagen, you can take a train from Copenhagen Central Station to Helsingør. The journey takes about 45 minutes. From the Helsingør train station, it's a short walk to the castle. The scenic route along the waterfront is pleasant and gives you beautiful views of the strait.

Entrance to Kronborg Castle is not free; you will need to buy a ticket. The price is reasonable and includes access to all the main areas of the castle. Be sure to check the castle's website for current ticket prices and opening hours, as these can vary.

When visiting Kronborg Castle, take your time to enjoy the surroundings. The castle's location offers stunning views of the water, and the surrounding area has lovely parks and gardens where you can relax after your tour. The castle grounds are also perfect for a leisurely stroll.

If you're a fan of history or literature, Kronborg Castle is an unforgettable experience. Its rich history and literary connections make it a unique place to visit, and exploring the castle will give you a deep appreciation for Denmark's cultural heritage.

Roskilde: The Viking Ship Museum and Cathedral

Roskilde, a charming city just a short train ride from Copenhagen, is home to two incredible attractions: the Viking Ship Museum and the Roskilde Cathedral. Both offer fascinating insights into Denmark's past and are well worth a visit.

The Viking Ship Museum is a must-see for anyone interested in Viking history. This museum is dedicated to the ships that the Vikings used to sail across the seas. When you arrive, you'll see several original Viking ships displayed in a large, airy hall. These ships were discovered in the nearby Roskilde Fjord and have been carefully preserved.

At the museum, you can explore the ships up close and learn about how they were built and used. There are also interactive exhibits where you can try your hand at Viking-era crafts and activities. One of the highlights is the chance to see a Viking ship being reconstructed. You can even join a boat trip on a replica Viking ship, which gives you a feel for what it was like to sail in these ancient vessels.

To get to the Viking Ship Museum from Copenhagen, you can take a train from Copenhagen Central Station to Roskilde. The journey takes about 25 minutes. From the train station, it's a short walk to the museum. The museum is well-signposted, and the walk along the scenic Roskilde Fjord is pleasant.

The Roskilde Cathedral, another significant attraction, is just a short distance from the Viking Ship Museum. This cathedral is a UNESCO World Heritage Site and is known for its stunning architecture. It's a grand building with intricate details and a rich history.

Inside the cathedral, you'll find beautiful stained glass windows and elaborate tombs of Danish royalty. The cathedral has been the burial place for many Danish kings and queens, making it an important historical site. The architecture is a mix of Gothic and Romanesque styles, reflecting the long history of the building.

To reach the Roskilde Cathedral from the Viking Ship Museum, just walk along the charming streets of Roskilde. The cathedral is situated in the heart of the city and is easy to find. Entrance to the cathedral usually requires a small fee, which helps support its maintenance.

When visiting Roskilde, take your time to explore both the Viking Ship Museum and the cathedral. The city itself is lovely, with quaint streets and local shops, so it's worth spending some extra time walking around and enjoying the atmosphere. Both attractions provide a deep dive into Denmark's rich history and are highlights of any trip to the region.

Malmö, Sweden: A Quick Trip Across the Øresund Bridge

Malmö, Sweden, is a fantastic destination just a short trip from Copenhagen, easily reached by crossing the Øresund Bridge. This bridge, which connects Denmark and Sweden, makes Malmö an accessible and exciting day trip from Copenhagen.

As soon as you arrive in Malmö, you'll notice its charming mix of old and new. The city is known for its beautiful parks, modern architecture, and historic buildings. One of the first places you might want to visit is the Lilla Torg, a lively square filled with cafes and restaurants. Here, you can sit outside and enjoy a coffee or a meal while watching the world go by.

Another must-see is Malmö's Turning Torso, a striking skyscraper that twists as it rises. It's one of the tallest buildings in Sweden and an architectural marvel. You can't go inside the building, but it's worth seeing from the outside. The nearby Västra Hamnen area, where the Turning Torso is located, is great for a leisurely stroll along the waterfront.

If you're interested in history, head to Malmöhus Castle. This 16th-century fortress houses several museums, including the Malmö Art Museum and the City Museum. The castle itself is a beautiful example of Renaissance architecture and offers a glimpse into the city's past. The surrounding park is also a pleasant place to relax.

For a taste of Malmö's vibrant culture, visit the Möllevången district. This area is known for its multicultural vibe and bustling market. It's a great spot to explore if you're looking for unique shops, international cuisine, and a lively atmosphere.

Getting to Malmö from Copenhagen is straightforward. You can take a train from Copenhagen Central Station directly to Malmö. The journey across the Øresund Bridge takes about 35 minutes. Once you arrive in Malmö's central station, it's easy to walk or take a local bus to the city's main attractions.

Malmö is also known for its green spaces. The Pildammsparken park is a large, scenic area where you can take a leisurely walk, have a picnic, or just enjoy the natural surroundings. It's a lovely spot to unwind and take in the fresh air.

Whether you're interested in modern architecture, historical sites, or just enjoying a different city for the day, Malmö has something to offer. It's a city that combines a relaxed atmosphere with interesting sights and activities, making it a perfect day trip from Copenhagen.

Dragør: A Charming Village Near the Sea

Dragør is a delightful village located just a short drive from Copenhagen, right by the sea. This picturesque spot is perfect for a peaceful escape from the city, offering a charming blend of old-world charm and coastal beauty.

When you arrive in Dragør, you'll immediately notice its well-preserved historical buildings. The village is known for its lovely, narrow streets lined with colorful, traditional houses. Walking around, you'll feel like you've stepped back in time. The houses, with their yellow and white facades, add a warm and inviting atmosphere to the village.

One of the main attractions in Dragør is the old harbor. It's a quaint and scenic area where you can see fishing boats bobbing in the water. There are also cozy cafes and restaurants here where you can enjoy a meal while watching the boats and taking in the sea breeze. It's a great spot for a leisurely lunch or a coffee break.

The Dragør Museum is another interesting place to visit. Located in a historic building, the museum offers insights into the village's history and maritime heritage. It's a small but fascinating museum where you can learn about Dragør's past, including its role as a fishing village and its development over the years.

If you enjoy walking or cycling, Dragør has some beautiful paths along the coastline. These paths provide stunning views of the sea and are perfect for a relaxing stroll or a bike ride.

The fresh air and serene surroundings make it a refreshing experience.

Another highlight of Dragør is its local market, held regularly in the village square. Here, you can find fresh produce, local crafts, and homemade treats. It's a lovely way to experience the local culture and pick up some unique souvenirs.

Getting to Dragør from Copenhagen is easy. You can take a bus or drive, and the journey takes about 30 minutes. The village is close enough to the city that it makes for a convenient day trip, but it feels like a world away with its tranquil atmosphere and scenic views.

In summary, Dragør is a charming village with its historical houses, scenic harbor, and relaxing coastal walks. It's an ideal spot for a quiet day out, offering a glimpse into Danish village life and the beauty of the sea. If you're looking for a peaceful retreat from the hustle and bustle of Copenhagen, Dragør is definitely worth a visit.

The Louisiana Museum of Modern Art: Art and Nature

The Louisiana Museum of Modern Art is a fantastic place to visit, located just north of Copenhagen. The museum beautifully combines modern art with stunning natural surroundings, making it a unique and enjoyable experience.

When you arrive at the Louisiana Museum, you'll be struck by its beautiful setting. The museum is situated right by the sea, with expansive gardens that blend seamlessly with the art inside. The views of the water and the lush green grounds make for a peaceful and inspiring environment.

The museum's collection includes a wide range of modern and contemporary art. Inside, you'll find works by famous artists like Picasso, Warhol, and Hockney, alongside pieces from Danish and international artists. The exhibitions change regularly, so there's always something new to see. The museum does a great job of showcasing art in a way that is accessible and engaging, whether you are a seasoned art lover or a casual visitor.

One of the highlights of visiting the Louisiana Museum is exploring the outdoor sculptures and the surrounding gardens. The grounds are dotted with impressive sculptures and installations that make a lovely complement to the art inside. The paths through the gardens offer beautiful views of the Øresund Strait and the nearby Swedish coastline.

The museum also has a cozy café where you can relax and enjoy a meal or a cup of coffee. The café offers a range of tasty options, from light snacks to more substantial meals. It's a nice place to take a break and soak in the beautiful surroundings.

To get to the Louisiana Museum of Modern Art, you can take a train from Copenhagen to Humlebæk Station, which is about a 40-minute ride. From the station, it's a short walk or a quick shuttle ride to the museum. If you prefer to drive, there is parking available at the museum.

The museum charges an entrance fee, but it is worth it for the experience you'll have. The combination of art and nature creates a special atmosphere that makes the visit memorable.

Overall, the Louisiana Museum of Modern Art is a wonderful destination that offers both cultural enrichment and natural beauty. If you're in the Copenhagen area and enjoy modern art, this museum is definitely worth a visit.

CHAPTER 9.
OUTDOOR ACTIVITIES

Copenhagen's Parks and Gardens

Copenhagen's parks and gardens offer lovely escapes into nature right in the heart of the city. Each place has its own unique charm and provides a perfect setting for relaxation, exploration, and enjoyment.

First, there's the King's Garden, located at Øster Voldgade 4A, 1350 Copenhagen. This is one of the most popular parks in the city, and it's easy to see why. The garden is beautifully designed with neatly trimmed lawns, colorful flowerbeds, and statues scattered throughout. It's the perfect spot for a leisurely walk or a picnic on a sunny day. The garden also surrounds the Rosenborg Castle, so you can combine a visit to both. To get there, you can take the metro to Nørreport Station and walk a short distance. The entrance is free, and it's a great place to unwind and enjoy the greenery.

Next on the list is the Botanical Garden, found at Gothersgade 128, 1350 Copenhagen. This garden is a haven for plant enthusiasts and anyone looking to escape the city's hustle. It features a vast collection of plants from around the world, housed in several greenhouses. The Victorian-style Palm House is particularly striking with its intricate ironwork and tropical plants. The garden also has lovely walking paths and tranquil spots where you can relax. To reach the Botanical Garden, you can take the metro to Nørreport Station and walk a bit from there. Admission is free, though some special exhibitions might have a fee.

Another gem is Frederiksberg Gardens, located at Frederiksberg Runddel, 2000 Frederiksberg. This park is known for its romantic landscape design, including picturesque lakes, winding paths, and charming bridges. It's a great place to take a relaxing stroll or enjoy a boat ride on the lake. The park is also home to the Copenhagen Zoo, so if you're interested, you can visit both in one trip. To get there, you can take the metro to Frederiksberg Station and walk to the park. The entrance to the park is free, and it's a wonderful spot for families and nature lovers alike.

Lastly, don't miss out on the Superkilen Park at Nørrebro. This park is quite different from the others as it's designed to celebrate diversity and features vibrant and modern designs. The park has unique installations and artwork from different cultures, creating a lively and colorful environment. It's a great place to experience a different side of Copenhagen and enjoy some outdoor activities. You can get to Superkilen Park by taking the metro to Nørrebro Station and walking a short distance. The park is free to visit and offers a fun and engaging experience.

Copenhagen's parks and gardens provide a range of experiences, from historic charm to modern vibrancy. Each location offers something special, whether it's a quiet place to relax or a space to explore nature and art. Make sure to visit these spots to enjoy the green side of Copenhagen and get a taste of its outdoor beauty.

Cycling in Copenhagen: Routes and Bike Rentals

Cycling in Copenhagen is one of the best ways to explore the city. The city is known for its bike-friendly streets and extensive network of cycling paths. Renting a bike and hitting the roads is not just a practical way to get around but also a fun way to see Copenhagen.

For bike rentals, you can start at a popular spot like Donkey Republic, which has several locations around the city, including one at Vesterbrogade 26, 1620 Copenhagen. This bike rental service is known for its easy-to-use app that lets you find and unlock bikes. The prices are reasonable, and you can rent bikes by the hour, day, or week, depending on your needs. To get there, you can take the train or metro to Vesterport Station and walk to the rental location.

Another option is the City Bikes service available at multiple spots, including one near Rådhuspladsen (City Hall Square) at Rådhuspladsen 1, 1550 Copenhagen. This is a convenient choice since it is centrally located. City Bikes operates a network of bike stations where you can pick up and drop off bikes. The rental is typically for a short period, making it ideal for quick trips around the city.

As for cycling routes, Copenhagen offers several scenic paths that cater to all levels of cyclists. One of the most enjoyable routes is along the waterfront, taking you through areas like Islands Brygge and the picturesque Nyhavn. This route is flat and easy, providing beautiful views of the harbor and lively city life. You can start your ride at the beginning of Nyhavn, located at Nyhavn 1-71, 1051 Copenhagen.

Another great route is the Lakes Route, which circles around the three main lakes in the city: Søerne. This route provides a more tranquil experience as you cycle past serene lakeside paths and beautiful parks. You can start at the park area near the Copenhagen Botanical Garden, located at Gothersgade 128, 1350 Copenhagen.

If you're up for a longer ride, consider heading to the bicycle path that leads to Amager Beach Park. The route offers a refreshing view of the sea and a chance to enjoy the sandy beach. Amager Beach Park is located at Amager Strandvej 401, 2300 Copenhagen. The park is a fantastic place to relax after a ride and enjoy a picnic or take a dip in the water.

Cycling in Copenhagen is not only efficient but also offers a fantastic way to experience the city's charm. The bike lanes are well-marked, and the city's bike infrastructure makes it easy to navigate. Whether you're cruising along the waterfront, exploring the lakes, or heading to the beach, biking through Copenhagen will give you a memorable and enjoyable experience of the city.

Canal Tours: Discovering the City from the Water

Taking a canal tour in Copenhagen is a fantastic way to see the city from a different perspective. The city's canals offer a unique view of its beautiful architecture, charming neighborhoods, and lively atmosphere.

One of the most popular options for canal tours is offered by Stromma. Their boats start at Nyhavn, which is located at Nyhavn 1-71, 1051 Copenhagen. This area is easy to reach by public transportation; you can take the metro to Kongens Nytorv Station and walk to Nyhavn. Stromma's canal tours run frequently throughout the day, and you can choose from different types of tours. They offer both guided tours in multiple languages and hop-on-hop-off options that let you explore various parts of the city at your own pace. The tour usually lasts around an hour and covers major sights like the Little Mermaid statue, Amalienborg Palace, and the modern buildings of the Copenhagen Opera House.

Another great option is the Canal Tours Copenhagen, which also departs from Nyhavn, specifically from the landing stage at Nyhavn 33, 1051 Copenhagen. This tour provides a comprehensive look at Copenhagen's waterfront and historical sites. Their boats are comfortable and offer both indoor and outdoor seating, making it a pleasant experience no matter the weather. The guides are knowledgeable and provide interesting commentary about the city's history and landmarks.

For a more intimate experience, you might consider a private tour. Private tours can be arranged through various companies, and they offer a chance to explore the canals with a smaller group. One company that provides this service is CPHT, located at Gammel Strand 24, 1202 Copenhagen. They offer customizable tours that can focus on specific interests, whether it's architecture, history, or just a leisurely ride through the city.

During your canal tour, you'll pass by many of Copenhagen's iconic sites. The boat will glide past the colorful facades of Nyhavn, the impressive buildings of Christianshavn, and the lush greenery of the King's Garden. You'll also get a unique view of the city's modern architecture along the waterfront. Keep your camera ready for shots of the Little Mermaid statue from the water and the picturesque harborside.

A canal tour is not just about sightseeing; it's also a relaxing way to spend a few hours. The gentle sway of the boat and the scenic views provide a peaceful break from the hustle and bustle of the city. Whether you're interested in learning more about Copenhagen's history or simply enjoying the beautiful surroundings, a canal tour is a delightful way to discover the city from the water.

The Beaches: Amager Strandpark and Beyond

Copenhagen offers some lovely beach spots where you can relax, swim, and enjoy the sunshine. Amager Strandpark is the most popular beach destination in the city, and it's well worth a visit.

Amager Strandpark is located at Amager Strandvej 100, 2300 Copenhagen. To get there, you can take the metro to Amager Strand Station. From there, it's a short walk to the beach. The park is a large area with a wide sandy beach, grassy areas for picnicking, and even a lagoon. It's perfect for a day out, whether you want to sunbathe, take a dip in the water, or have a picnic. There are also walking and cycling paths if you want to explore the area more. The views of the Øresund Strait are beautiful, especially at sunset.

In addition to Amager Strandpark, Copenhagen has other nice spots for beach lovers. If you're looking for something a bit different, you might want to check out Bellevue Beach. Bellevue Beach is located at Bellevuevej 9, 2900 Hellerup. To get there, you can take the S-train to Klampenborg Station, and then it's just a short walk to the beach. Bellevue Beach is known for its clean sand and beautiful architecture along the shore. It's a bit quieter than Amager Strandpark and has a more relaxed atmosphere.

Another great beach option is the Harbor Bath at Islands Brygge. This is a unique spot where you can swim right in the heart of the city. It's located at Islands Brygge 20, 2300

Copenhagen. The harbor bath has several swimming pools with different depths and temperatures, making it a fantastic place for a swim. The area around the harbor bath is also great for lounging, with plenty of space to relax and enjoy the views of the city.

For a more local experience, you might want to visit the beach at Kastrup Søbad. This beach is located at Kastrup Strandpark, 2770 Kastrup, and is accessible by taking the metro to Kastrup Station. The beach has a relaxed vibe and offers stunning views of the water. It's a bit off the beaten path, making it a nice spot if you're looking for a quieter place to unwind.

All these beaches provide a great way to enjoy Copenhagen's beautiful summer weather. Whether you want to swim, sunbathe, or simply take a stroll along the shore, these spots offer something for everyone. So grab your beach gear and head to one of these lovely locations for a refreshing day by the water.

Exploring Copenhagen's Islands: Refshaleøen and Paper Island

Copenhagen's islands offer a unique perspective of the city, showcasing a mix of modern culture and historical charm. Refshaleøen and Paper Island are two must-visit spots that will give you a memorable experience.

Refshaleøen is an island with a vibrant and evolving atmosphere. It's located just a short trip from the city center at Refshaleøen, 1432 Copenhagen. To get there, you can take the bus or bike, as it's a bit of a distance from the nearest metro station. Alternatively, a pleasant walk from the main city area or a short boat ride offers a unique view of the city.

Once you arrive, you'll notice Refshaleøen is known for its lively cultural scene. The island used to be an industrial area, but it has transformed into a hub for creativity and innovation. You'll find a variety of things to do here. The street food market, Reffen, is a highlight. It's a bustling place with a diverse range of food stalls offering everything from gourmet dishes to simple snacks. It's a great spot to sample different cuisines while enjoying the waterfront views.

Refshaleøen is also home to several art installations and workshops. You can explore the local art scene, visit galleries, or even participate in workshops if you're interested in getting hands-on with some creative projects. The island has a relaxed vibe, and wandering through it is an experience in itself. The industrial architecture mixed with modern developments makes for an interesting backdrop.

Paper Island, known locally as Papirøen, is another fascinating destination. It's located at Trangravsvej 14, 1436 Copenhagen. To get there, you can easily walk or cycle from the city center, or take a short boat ride. The island is a bit quieter compared to Refshaleøen but offers its own charm.

Paper Island was once the site of a large paper warehouse, but now it's famous for its food market. The area has recently been redeveloped into a cultural space with a mix of restaurants, shops, and recreational areas. You'll find a range of dining options, from trendy cafes to cozy eateries. The atmosphere is laid-back, perfect for a leisurely afternoon.

Both islands provide different yet complementary experiences. Refshaleøen is energetic and creative, while Paper Island offers a more relaxed, culinary-focused experience. Exploring these islands will give you a deeper appreciation of Copenhagen's innovative spirit and its commitment to blending old and new. Whether you're enjoying a meal at Reffen, exploring art galleries, or simply taking in the views, these islands are a great addition to any Copenhagen itinerary.

CHAPTER 10.
COPENHAGEN FOR DIFFERENT TRAVELERS

Copenhagen with Kids: Family-Friendly Activities

Copenhagen is a fantastic city for families with kids, offering a variety of fun and engaging activities that everyone will enjoy. Whether you're looking for outdoor adventures, interactive museums, or charming attractions, there's something for every family in this vibrant city.

One of the best places to start is Tivoli Gardens. Located in the heart of the city at Vesterbrogade 3, 1630 Copenhagen, Tivoli is an amusement park and garden that has been entertaining visitors since 1843. It's like stepping into a magical world with its beautiful rides, games, and shows. There are roller coasters, carousels, and plenty of space to explore. During the summer, Tivoli also hosts concerts and special events, making it a lively place for families to spend the day.

Another great spot is the Copenhagen Zoo. Situated at Roskildevej 32, 2000 Frederiksberg, it's easy to reach by bus or metro. The zoo is home to a wide variety of animals, including lions, elephants, and penguins. Kids will love the chance to see their favorite animals up close. There are also playgrounds and picnic areas where families can take a break and enjoy a meal together.

For a more hands-on experience, the Experimentarium is a must-visit. Located at Lautrupbjerg 1, 2750 Ballerup, it's a bit outside the city center but well worth the trip. The museum is full of interactive exhibits and experiments that make learning fun. From exploring the human body to playing with light and sound, there are plenty of activities to keep kids entertained and engaged.

The National Aquarium Denmark, known as Den Blå Planet, is another exciting destination. Located at Jakob Fortlingsvej 1, 2770 Kastrup, it's easily accessible by metro. The aquarium features impressive displays of marine life, including sharks, rays, and colorful fish. There are also touch pools where kids can get hands-on with sea creatures and educational exhibits that teach about ocean conservation.

If you're looking for something a bit different, consider visiting the Copenhagen Botanical Garden at Gothersgade 128, 1123 Copenhagen. While it's not specifically designed for kids, the beautiful gardens and impressive greenhouse are a peaceful place to explore. Kids can enjoy running around the open spaces and spotting different plants and flowers.

Copenhagen also has several family-friendly parks and playgrounds. One of the best is Frederiksberg Gardens, located at Frederiksberg Runddel, 2000 Frederiksberg. The park features spacious lawns, a lake with swan boats, and a large playground. It's a great spot for a relaxing day out where kids can play and parents can enjoy the peaceful surroundings.

Overall, Copenhagen offers a wide range of activities that cater to families with kids. From thrilling rides at Tivoli Gardens to interactive exhibits at the Experimentarium, there's no shortage of fun things to do. With its welcoming atmosphere and diverse attractions, Copenhagen is a wonderful city for a family adventure.

Romantic Copenhagen: Couples' Getaway

Copenhagen is a perfect city for a romantic getaway, offering a mix of charming spots and cozy experiences that couples will love. Whether you're strolling along scenic canals or enjoying a candlelit dinner, there's no shortage of romantic activities in this beautiful city.

Start your day with a peaceful walk along Nyhavn, one of Copenhagen's most picturesque areas. The colorful buildings and historic ships create a charming backdrop for a leisurely stroll. You can stop at one of the many cafés lining the canal for a coffee or pastry while soaking in the view. If you're feeling adventurous, consider taking a canal tour from here. The boat ride offers a unique perspective of the city and its landmarks, making it a special experience for couples.

Another romantic spot is the King's Garden, located at Gothersgade 128, 1123 Copenhagen. This beautiful park is perfect for a relaxing afternoon. You can wander through the lush gardens, find a quiet bench to sit and chat, or even have a picnic on the grass. The park is home to Rosenborg Castle, which adds a touch of history to your visit. The castle's picturesque surroundings make for a lovely backdrop, especially in the spring and summer when the flowers are in full bloom.

For a memorable dining experience, head to one of Copenhagen's intimate restaurants. Places like Restaurant Radio, located at Julius Thomsens Gade 12, 1925 Copenhagen, offer a cozy atmosphere and delicious food. The menu often features local and seasonal ingredients, and the staff provides excellent service. Sharing a meal here can be a delightful way to spend time together.

In the evening, you might enjoy a romantic boat ride on the canals. The gentle sway of the boat and the soft city lights create a serene setting. There are several companies offering private tours, so you can have a more intimate experience. It's a wonderful way to see Copenhagen from a different angle and enjoy some quiet time together.

Another option is to visit Tivoli Gardens at Vesterbrogade 3, 1630 Copenhagen. This historic amusement park transforms into a magical place in the evening with its beautiful lights and lively atmosphere. You can take a romantic ride on the Ferris wheel, stroll through the gardens, or enjoy one of the many shows or concerts that take place there.

If you're looking for a special treat, consider a visit to one of Copenhagen's charming bakeries or chocolatiers. Places like A. C. Perch's Thehandel, located at Kronprinsensgade 5, 1114 Copenhagen, offer a range of delicious chocolates and pastries. Sharing a sweet treat together can be a delightful way to end your day.

Copenhagen's romantic side is also evident in its cozy and stylish hotels. Many offer beautiful rooms with views of the city or the canals, perfect for a romantic stay. A stay at a boutique hotel like Hotel SP34, located at Sankt Peders Stræde 34, 1453 Copenhagen, provides a blend of modern comfort and charm.

Overall, Copenhagen offers a range of romantic experiences that cater to different tastes and interests. From scenic walks and intimate dinners to charming boat rides and cozy stays, there's something to make your couples' getaway truly special.

Copenhagen for Solo Travelers: Safe and Fun

Copenhagen is a fantastic city for solo travelers, offering a blend of safety, friendliness, and exciting activities. Whether you're exploring historic sites, enjoying local cuisine, or simply soaking in the city's vibrant atmosphere, there are plenty of experiences to enjoy on your own.

Begin your adventure by exploring the city center. Copenhagen is known for being very safe, with friendly locals who are often happy to help if you need directions or recommendations. The city is also very walkable, so you can easily navigate through its charming streets and squares.

A must-see is Nyhavn, with its colorful buildings and historic boats. Stroll along the canal and grab a coffee or a bite to eat at one of the many cafés. The atmosphere is lively and welcoming, making it a great place to people-watch and relax. If you're interested in history, consider taking a canal tour from Nyhavn. It's a relaxing way to see the city and learn about its landmarks.

Another great spot is the Tivoli Gardens. Located at Vesterbrogade 3, 1630 Copenhagen, this amusement park is not just for families. It has beautiful gardens, charming rides, and various entertainment options. Whether you want to enjoy a ride on the Ferris wheel or simply walk around and take in the lights and decorations, Tivoli offers a fun experience for solo travelers.

For a bit of culture, visit the National Museum of Denmark, located at Ny Vestergade 10, 1471 Copenhagen. This museum provides a deep dive into Danish history and culture. You can spend hours exploring the exhibits, which range from ancient artifacts to displays about Danish life. It's a great way to learn more about the country and its past.

If you enjoy art, the Louisiana Museum of Modern Art is another highlight. Located at Gl. Strandvej 13, 3050 Humlebæk, just a short train ride from Copenhagen, it's a beautiful place to see contemporary art set against a stunning backdrop of nature. The museum's location by the water and its impressive collection make for a peaceful and inspiring visit.

Copenhagen is also known for its bike-friendly environment. Renting a bike is a fantastic way to see the city. There are many bike rental shops throughout the city. One good option is Baisikeli, located at Nørrebrogade 90, 2200 Copenhagen. Cycling through the city lets you see more in less time and gives you the freedom to explore at your own pace.

For solo travelers who enjoy meeting new people, consider joining a group tour or a local event. Copenhagen has various walking tours, cooking classes, and social events that can be a great way to connect with others and make new friends. Websites like Meetup or local tourist information centers can help you find these opportunities.

Safety is always a priority for solo travelers. Copenhagen is generally very safe, but it's always wise to take usual precautions. Keep an eye on your belongings, especially in crowded areas, and be cautious when exploring unfamiliar parts of the city after dark.

Copenhagen offers a range of activities and experiences for solo travelers. From its welcoming atmosphere and easy navigation to its rich cultural offerings and friendly locals, it's a city where you can easily enjoy your own company while discovering new and exciting things.

CHAPTER 11.
SUSTAINABLE TRAVEL IN COPENHAGEN

Eco-Friendly Accommodation

Exploring Copenhagen with a focus on eco-friendly accommodation offers a unique blend of sustainability and comfort. When I visited, I sought out places that align with green principles, and I was impressed by how the city integrates environmental consciousness into its hospitality sector.

One standout option is the Hotel Alexandra, located at H.C. Andersens Boulevard 8, 1553 Copenhagen. This hotel not only combines classic Danish charm with modern sustainability practices but also has an impressive collection of retro Danish furniture, which adds a nostalgic touch to the stay. The Hotel Alexandra emphasizes eco-friendly operations, such as energy-efficient systems and waste reduction practices. To get there, simply take the Metro to the Kongens Nytorv station, which is a short walk from the hotel.

During my stay, I appreciated the hotel's commitment to reducing its carbon footprint while providing exceptional service. The staff was incredibly friendly and knowledgeable about local eco-friendly initiatives, which was a great touch. For breakfast, they offered locally sourced and organic options, making it easy to start the day on a sustainable note.

Another excellent choice is the Nimb Hotel, situated at Bernstorffsgade 5, 1577 Copenhagen. This hotel is part of the larger Tivoli Gardens complex and is renowned for its commitment to sustainability. Nimb Hotel has implemented a range of green practices, including energy-efficient lighting and water-saving measures. To reach Nimb Hotel, take the Metro to the Tivoli Gardens station, which is conveniently close.

I enjoyed the hotel's lush, green surroundings and the emphasis on incorporating eco-friendly practices into their luxurious service. The gardens around the hotel are beautifully maintained, and the emphasis on natural elements adds to the overall experience. Staying here felt like a blend of comfort and environmental responsibility.

For a more budget-conscious option, check out the Urban House Copenhagen by MEININGER at H.C. Andersens Boulevard 50, 1553 Copenhagen. This eco-conscious hostel focuses on sustainable living with features like energy-saving systems and waste sorting. It's also conveniently located near the Central Station, making it easy to get around the city.

During my stay at Urban House, I was impressed by the modern, clean facilities and the friendly atmosphere. The hostel's commitment to sustainability was evident in every detail, from the eco-friendly cleaning products to the organic breakfast options. It's a fantastic choice for travelers who want to be environmentally responsible without breaking the bank.

If you're looking for a unique eco-friendly stay, consider booking a room at the Zleep Hotel Copenhagen Arena, located at Hannemanns Allé 51, 2300 Copenhagen. This hotel is known for its green certifications and has incorporated various eco-friendly measures into its operations. The hotel is easily accessible via the Metro to the Ørestad station, which is a short walk away.

My experience at Zleep Hotel was quite enjoyable. The emphasis on sustainability was apparent throughout my stay, and I appreciated the eco-conscious amenities provided. The rooms were comfortable, and the hotel's location near the Bella Center made it convenient for attending conferences and events.

Copenhagen's commitment to sustainability extends beyond these accommodations, as the city is full of green spaces and eco-friendly initiatives. By choosing eco-friendly lodging, you contribute to a larger movement towards environmental responsibility while enjoying the charm and beauty of Copenhagen.

Green Transportation: Biking, Walking, and Public Transit

Copenhagen is a city that makes green transportation easy and enjoyable. Whether you're biking, walking, or using public transit, you'll find plenty of options to get around while being kind to the environment.

Biking is a fantastic way to explore Copenhagen. The city is famous for its bike-friendly infrastructure, with dedicated bike lanes and bike-friendly traffic signals. To rent a bike, you can use the Bycyklen service. You'll find bike stations all over the city. For example, you can pick up a bike at a station on Rådhuspladsen, which is a central area and very convenient. Riding a bike lets you easily navigate through charming neighborhoods and scenic spots, and you'll find plenty of bike racks to park your bike.

Walking is another excellent way to experience Copenhagen. The city center is compact, so many attractions are within walking distance of each other. Strolling along the streets gives you a chance to discover hidden gems like cozy cafes and unique shops. You can take a leisurely walk along Strøget, one of the longest pedestrian streets in Europe. Walking lets you soak in the city's atmosphere and enjoy its beautiful architecture at your own pace.

Public transit in Copenhagen is efficient and eco-friendly. The Metro system is quick and connects you to major parts of the city, including the airport. The Metro stations are clean and easy to navigate, with clear signs and announcements in both Danish and English. You can get a City Pass or a Rejsekort card for unlimited rides or pay for single tickets as needed.

Buses are also a great option, and they cover areas that the Metro doesn't reach. The buses are modern and equipped with bike racks, making it easy to combine biking and public transit.

Trains connect Copenhagen to other cities and towns in Denmark, and many are operated with eco-friendly practices. The train station at Københavns Hovedbanegård is well-located and offers easy connections to various destinations.

Using green transportation in Copenhagen not only helps reduce your carbon footprint but also enhances your experience of the city. It's easy to get around, and you'll find that each mode of transport offers a different way to see and enjoy Copenhagen.

Sustainable Dining: Organic and Locally Sourced Food

Sustainable dining in Copenhagen is all about enjoying delicious food while supporting the environment and local farmers. Many restaurants focus on organic and locally sourced ingredients, making it easy for you to eat well and feel good about your choices.

One popular place to start is at restaurants that specialize in organic food. For instance, you can visit a spot like BioMio, located on Vesterbrogade. This restaurant prides itself on serving dishes made with organic ingredients, from vegetables to meats. You'll find that the menu changes with the seasons, which means you're always getting the freshest, most local produce available. The atmosphere is relaxed, and the food is flavorful and satisfying.

Another great option is to check out Smørrebrød spots that use local ingredients. Smørrebrød is Denmark's traditional open-faced sandwich, and many places now offer versions with organic and locally sourced toppings. Places like Aamanns 1921 on Østerbro are known for their commitment to high-quality, sustainable ingredients. Their smørrebrød is not only delicious but also crafted with care to support local farmers and producers.

If you're interested in farm-to-table dining, visit a restaurant like Manfreds, located on Jægersborggade. They focus on serving dishes made with ingredients from local farms, and they often have a menu that changes based on what's fresh and in season. The food is prepared with a lot of attention to detail, and you'll experience a range of flavors that highlight the best of Danish produce.

For a more casual dining experience, try out local markets and food halls. Places like Torvehallerne on Frederiksberg offer a variety of stalls where you can find fresh, organic produce and locally made products. It's a great spot to sample different foods, from cheeses and meats to pastries and salads, all made with a focus on sustainability.

In Copenhagen, you'll also find that many restaurants and cafes are committed to reducing waste. They often use eco-friendly packaging and encourage customers to bring their own reusable containers. This commitment to sustainability is part of the city's broader effort to make dining out both enjoyable and environmentally friendly.

By choosing restaurants and markets that focus on organic and locally sourced food, you're not only enjoying great meals but also supporting practices that are better for the planet. It's an easy way to make a positive impact while experiencing the best of Copenhagen's culinary scene.

Responsible Tourism: Minimizing Your Footprint

Responsible tourism is all about traveling in a way that has a positive impact on the places you visit and minimizes any harm to the environment and local communities. Here's how you can be a responsible traveler and make a difference while enjoying your trip.

First, start by planning your trip with sustainability in mind. Choose destinations that are committed to preserving their natural beauty and cultural heritage. Look for accommodations and tour operators that have eco-friendly practices, such as reducing waste, conserving energy, and supporting local businesses. Many places now offer eco-certified options, so you can make choices that align with responsible tourism.

When you arrive at your destination, be mindful of your environmental impact. Opt for public transportation, biking, or walking instead of renting a car. This helps reduce pollution and minimizes your carbon footprint. Many cities have excellent public transit systems and bike-sharing programs that make getting around easy and sustainable.

When staying in hotels or other accommodations, practice energy conservation. Turn off lights and unplug electronics when you're not using them. Reduce water usage by taking shorter showers and reusing towels. These small actions can collectively make a big difference in reducing your environmental impact.

Support local communities by buying goods and services from local businesses. Eat at locally-owned restaurants, shop at markets, and stay in accommodations run by locals. This helps ensure that the money you spend benefits the community directly and supports local economies.

Be respectful of natural and cultural sites. Follow marked trails and avoid disturbing wildlife. Stick to designated areas and avoid leaving trash behind. Respect local customs and traditions, and always ask for permission before taking photos of people. This shows respect for the local culture and ensures that you're contributing positively to the places you visit.

One key aspect of responsible tourism is to leave no trace. Make sure to dispose of waste properly, recycle when possible, and avoid single-use plastics. Bring a reusable water bottle and shopping bag to reduce the amount of waste you produce. If you see litter while exploring, pick it up if you can.

Educate yourself about the local environment and culture before your trip. Understanding the challenges faced by the destination helps you make informed decisions and be a more responsible traveler. Many destinations offer information on their websites about how to travel responsibly, so take some time to read up before you go.

By taking these steps, you can help protect the places you visit and ensure that your travels have a positive impact. Responsible tourism not only enhances your travel experience but also contributes to the preservation of the environment and the well-being of local communities.

CHAPTER 12.
PRACTICAL INFORMATION

Currency and Budgeting: Navigating Danish Kroner

When planning a trip to Copenhagen, understanding how to manage your money effectively is crucial to making the most of your visit. Here's a detailed guide to help you navigate currency exchange and budgeting for your trip.

First, it's important to note that Copenhagen, like the rest of Denmark, uses the Danish Krone (DKK), not the Euro (€). While the Euro is widely accepted in many places, particularly in tourist areas, the Krone is the official currency. The Krone is significant as it represents Denmark's stable and robust economy. Understanding and using the local currency will help you avoid unnecessary fees and get the best value for your money.

For exchanging currency, you have several options. Banks are a reliable choice for exchanging money, though they may charge a small fee. Exchange offices, often found in tourist areas and major transport hubs, offer convenient services but might have higher fees or less favorable exchange rates. ATMs are a popular choice as they offer competitive exchange rates, but keep in mind that your bank might charge international withdrawal fees. To minimize costs, it's advisable to use ATMs with lower fees and to exchange larger sums at once if possible.

When budgeting for your trip, consider breaking down your expenses into different categories. For accommodation, you can find options ranging from budget hostels to luxury hotels. A budget hostel might cost around 150-200 DKK per night, while mid-range hotels can range from 800-1,500 DKK. Luxury hotels start from 2,000 DKK and can go up significantly from there.

Meals in Copenhagen vary in price. Budget travelers might spend around 100-150 DKK for a meal at a casual eatery or street food stall. Mid-range restaurants typically cost 200-400 DKK per person. For a more luxurious dining experience, expect to pay 500 DKK or more. Street food markets are a great way to enjoy local flavors on a budget, and you can often find tasty and affordable options.

Transportation costs include options like buses, trains, and taxis. A single bus or train ticket costs around 24-30 DKK, while taxis start at about 40 DKK and add up quickly. Many visitors find that biking is a cost-effective and enjoyable way to get around Copenhagen. Bike rentals generally cost between 100-150 DKK per day.

In terms of payment methods, credit and debit cards are widely accepted throughout Copenhagen. Visa and Mastercard are the most commonly used, though American Express might not be accepted everywhere. Local payment apps like MobilePay are popular, especially for smaller transactions. It's also wise to carry some cash, as smaller shops and markets might not accept cards.

Local pricing can vary, with tourist hotspots often being more expensive than local favorites. For instance, popular attractions and restaurants in the city center may have higher prices compared to those in less touristy areas. Seasonal variations also affect costs, with prices typically rising during peak tourist seasons like summer.

Reflecting on my own experience, I remember arriving in Copenhagen and realizing I had relied too much on my credit card. While most places accepted cards, I found that many local markets and smaller cafes preferred cash. After a few awkward moments of trying to figure out where to get cash, I learned to always carry a small amount of Krone for those smaller transactions. Using a budgeting app helped me keep track of my spending and avoid overshooting my budget.

To manage your finances efficiently, consider using budgeting apps like Trail Wallet or Mint to keep track of your expenses. Currency converter apps can also be handy for quick conversions between DKK and your home currency. Websites like XE.com offer up-to-date exchange rates and can help you make informed decisions.

By understanding the local currency, exploring your exchange options, budgeting wisely, and using the right payment methods, you'll be well-prepared to enjoy all that Copenhagen has to offer without any financial hiccups.

Language: Key Danish Phrases and English Proficiency

When traveling to Copenhagen, it's helpful to know a bit about the local languages and communication styles to make your visit smoother and more enjoyable.

In Copenhagen, the primary language spoken is Danish. However, English is widely understood, especially in tourist areas, hotels, and restaurants. Knowing a few essential Danish phrases can enhance your experience and show respect for the local culture.

For basic greetings and polite phrases, here are some useful Danish expressions along with their phonetic pronunciations:

- Hello: "Hej" (pronounced like "hi")
- Please: "Vær så venlig" (pronounced like "vair saw ven-lee")
- Thank you: "Tak" (pronounced like "tack")
- Excuse me: "Undskyld" (pronounced like "oon-skool")

In situations like ordering food, asking for directions, making purchases, and seeking assistance, these phrases will be particularly useful:

- How much does this cost?: "Hvor meget koster det?" (pronounced like "vor my-eth koster day?")
- I would like a coffee, please: "Jeg vil gerne have en kaffe, tak" (pronounced like "yai vil ger-ne ha en kaf-fe tak")
- Can you help me?: "Kan du hjælpe mig?" (pronounced like "kan doo yelp may?")
- Where is the nearest metro station?: "Hvor er den nærmeste metrostation?" (pronounced like "vor air den naerm-este may-tro stah-shun?")

To quickly learn these essential phrases, you might use mobile apps like Duolingo or Babbel, which offer language courses tailored to Danish. Phrasebooks and online tutorials can also be helpful. Websites like Memrise provide interactive learning tools that can be quite useful for picking up key phrases.

Cultural insights are important when interacting with locals. In Denmark, it's common to use informal language with people you meet in casual settings, while formal language is reserved for more official contexts. Politeness is appreciated, and a friendly tone can make interactions more pleasant. Danish people tend to value directness and clarity, so being straightforward while maintaining respect is key.

While Danish is the local language, many people in Copenhagen speak English, especially in places frequented by tourists. Most major attractions, hotels, and restaurants will have English-speaking staff. If you need assistance, don't hesitate to ask if they speak English, and you will likely find that they do.

Respecting the local language and culture by learning a few basic Danish phrases can greatly enhance your visit. It shows appreciation for the local community and can make your interactions more meaningful. Even if your Danish isn't perfect, locals will appreciate your effort to engage with their language and culture.

By being prepared with a few key phrases and understanding some cultural nuances, you'll find communicating in Copenhagen to be a rewarding part of your travel experience.

Safety and Health: Staying Safe in Copenhagen

Traveling to Copenhagen can be an exciting adventure, but it's important to stay mindful of safety and health to ensure a smooth and enjoyable trip. Here's a guide to help you navigate these aspects effectively.

When it comes to general safety, Copenhagen is known for being a safe city, but it's always wise to stay aware of your surroundings. Keep an eye on your belongings, especially in crowded areas like tourist attractions and public transport. Avoid walking alone late at night in less busy parts of town. Respect local customs and follow any advice from locals or your accommodation regarding areas to avoid or special safety precautions.

For outdoor activities, such as exploring the city's parks or cycling around, safety considerations are generally straightforward. If you're planning to venture out for a day trip or bike ride, check the weather forecast to avoid getting caught in unfavorable conditions. Copenhagen's trails and routes are well-marked, but make sure to stick to designated paths and follow any posted signs. If you're hiking outside the city, understand the trail difficulty and your own fitness level. While altitude sickness isn't a concern in Copenhagen, being prepared for changes in weather is essential, so dress in layers.

Health precautions are crucial for a comfortable trip. Copenhagen's climate can vary, so it's important to stay hydrated and use sunscreen, even on cloudy days. Layering your clothing helps you adjust to changing temperatures easily. No specific vaccinations are required for travel to

Copenhagen, but maintaining routine vaccinations is always a good practice. For any health advisories, you can check with health organizations or your travel advisor before your trip.

In case of an emergency, it's helpful to have important contact numbers handy. For local emergency services, dial 112, which covers police, fire, and ambulance services. Hospitals like Rigshospitalet, located at Blegdamsvej 9, 2100 Copenhagen, are well-equipped for medical emergencies. If you're engaged in outdoor activities and need specific rescue services, the Danish Red Cross and local rescue teams can be reached through the same emergency number.

Travel insurance is a must-have to cover unexpected events. Look for a policy that includes health coverage, emergency evacuations, and medical expenses. Ensure it covers activities you plan to do and that you understand the claim process in case you need to use it.

Local health services are readily available in Copenhagen. Pharmacies, known as "apotek," are scattered throughout the city and can provide medication and health advice. For minor health issues, you can visit a local clinic or hospital. Some clinics might require you to book an appointment in advance, so it's useful to know your options before you need them.

To stay informed and safe, consider using safety apps and local websites. Apps like "Copenhagen City Guide" can provide up-to-date information on local events and safety tips. Websites like VisitCopenhagen offer comprehensive travel advice and safety information.

By keeping these tips in mind, you'll be well-prepared to enjoy everything Copenhagen has to offer while prioritizing your safety and health.

Etiquette and Local Customs

When visiting Copenhagen, understanding local etiquette and customs will help you blend in smoothly and enhance your travel experience. Here are some key things to keep in mind.

Copenhagen is known for its friendly and polite people. Greeting someone with a warm smile and a handshake is common. When addressing someone, use their title and last name unless they invite you to use their first name. It's also polite to remove your shoes when entering someone's home, so be prepared for that if you're invited over.

In public places, Danes appreciate personal space and quiet. Keep your voice down on public transport and in public areas. It's considered rude to speak loudly on phones or have loud conversations in quiet places like cafes or libraries.

When dining out, tipping is not mandatory in Denmark as service charges are included in the bill. However, rounding up the bill or leaving a small tip is appreciated if you've received excellent service. In cafes and restaurants, it's common to wait to be seated, and you should wait for the staff to bring the bill rather than asking for it immediately.

If you're using public transportation, be sure to respect the local customs. Always queue for buses and trains, and let passengers disembark before you board. Priority seats are reserved for elderly, disabled, or pregnant passengers, so be considerate.

Cycling is very popular in Copenhagen, and you'll see many locals commuting by bike. If you rent a bike, remember to follow traffic rules and use bike lanes where available. Always signal your turns and be mindful of pedestrians.

When visiting attractions or cultural sites, dress modestly and follow any specific guidelines provided. For instance, if you visit a church, it's respectful to dress appropriately and maintain a quiet demeanor.

Danes are also known for their environmental consciousness. Recycling is a norm, so be sure to separate your waste properly. Look for the recycling bins labeled for paper, plastics, and other materials.

Understanding and respecting these local customs will help you have a more enjoyable and respectful stay in Copenhagen. The Danes are generally very welcoming, and making an effort to follow these practices will make your interactions smoother and more pleasant.

Useful Apps And Website

When traveling to Copenhagen, having the right apps on your phone can make your journey smoother and more enjoyable. Here's a guide to some essential apps that will help you navigate the city, find great places to stay and eat, and make the most of your trip.

For general travel needs, apps like Google Maps and Citymapper are indispensable. Google Maps helps you with navigation, public transport options, and finding nearby attractions. Citymapper provides detailed transit information, helping you plan routes using buses, trains, and the metro system. Both are excellent tools for getting around Copenhagen efficiently.

If you're planning to explore the outdoors or enjoy activities around Copenhagen, consider downloading hiking and outdoor apps like AllTrails, Gaia GPS, and ViewRanger. AllTrails offers detailed maps and reviews for hiking trails, making it easier to find the best routes. Gaia GPS is great for navigation and planning, while ViewRanger provides topographic maps and route tracking.

When it comes to finding a place to stay or dining options, apps like Booking.com, Airbnb, and TripAdvisor can be very useful. Booking.com allows you to compare hotel prices, read reviews, and book rooms directly. Airbnb offers a variety of accommodations, from unique stays to more traditional options. TripAdvisor is perfect for finding restaurants, cafes, and bars with user reviews and ratings to help you choose the best spots.

Language and translation apps can help you communicate more effectively. Google Translate is invaluable for translating signs, menus, and conversations. Duolingo can assist with learning some basic Danish phrases, which can be very helpful and appreciated by locals. iTranslate is another useful tool for translating text and speech in real-time.

In case of emergencies or if you need to stay safe, apps like First Aid by American Red Cross provide essential medical information and guidance. GeoSure Travel Safety offers insights into safety conditions and risks in different areas. Both apps can be reassuring to have on hand, especially if you find yourself in an unfamiliar situation.

To deepen your understanding of Copenhagen's culture and history, apps like Dolomiti UNESCO and Dolomiti Superski offer fascinating insights and guided tours. While these specific apps focus on the Dolomites, similar local cultural and historical apps can enhance your experience in Copenhagen by providing context and background on the city's landmarks and museums.

Since internet access might be limited in some areas, it's wise to download offline maps and guides. Google Maps, for instance, allows you to download maps for offline use, which can be very helpful if you find yourself without a reliable internet connection.

When using these apps, make sure your phone is fully charged and consider carrying a portable power bank to avoid running out of battery. Be mindful of data usage and roaming charges, especially if you're traveling internationally. Downloading apps and information before your trip can help you avoid unexpected charges and ensure you have access to all the tools you need.

By equipping yourself with these apps, you'll be well-prepared to navigate Copenhagen, discover its many attractions, and make the most of your visit to this vibrant city.

CONCLUSION

As your journey through Copenhagen comes to a close, it's impossible not to reflect on the distinctive charm and allure that this city offers. Copenhagen is a destination that blends the serene beauty of its natural landscapes with a vibrant cultural scene and a rich culinary tradition. Whether you're wandering through the colorful streets of Nyhavn, exploring the historical treasures at Rosenborg Castle, or cycling along the picturesque canals, there's something uniquely captivating about the way Copenhagen intertwines its history, culture, and modernity.

Copenhagen isn't just a place to visit; it's a place to experience deeply. It's about feeling the crisp air on your face as you cycle through the city, tasting the fresh seafood at a local harbor-side eatery, and hearing the soft hum of conversation in a cozy café as you sip on a perfectly brewed coffee. My own connection to Copenhagen has always been rooted in these small, yet profoundly meaningful, moments. Each visit offers a new perspective, a new discovery, and an ever-growing appreciation for the city's understated elegance and its ability to surprise and delight at every turn. There's something almost magical about how Copenhagen can make you feel both at home and entirely invigorated by the unfamiliar.

One of the greatest joys of travel is stepping outside your comfort zone, and Copenhagen offers countless opportunities to do just that. Whether you're challenging yourself with a hike in the surrounding natural parks, savoring a traditional Danish smørrebrød at a local diner, or engaging in a conversation with a friendly local, every new experience is a chance to grow and learn. These are the moments that often leave the most lasting impressions—the ones where you push past what you know and embrace the new and unexpected.

While Copenhagen's iconic sights are undoubtedly worth visiting, some of the city's most memorable experiences can be found off the beaten path. Venture beyond the well-trodden tourist spots and you'll find hidden gems like the quaint neighborhood of Christianshavn with its charming canals, or the serene beauty of the city's many parks and green spaces. Exploring these lesser-known areas not only allows you to connect more deeply with the local culture but also provides a sense of discovery that makes your journey uniquely your own.

As you explore Copenhagen, I encourage you to travel mindfully and sustainably. The city's commitment to green living is evident in its widespread use of bicycles, its focus on renewable energy, and its thriving organic food scene. By respecting the environment, supporting local businesses, and being considerate of the local community, you contribute to the preservation of this beautiful city for future generations of travelers.

Before you set out on your Copenhagen adventure, here are a few final tips to enhance your experience: Plan ahead, but leave room for spontaneity. Some of the best travel moments happen when you deviate from the plan and embrace the unexpected. Don't hesitate to ask locals for recommendations—they often have the best insights on where to go and what to see. And most importantly, allow yourself to fully immerse in the experience. Whether it's by savoring a quiet moment in a local park, taking in the city's vibrant street art, or simply enjoying the rhythm of everyday life, let Copenhagen's unique atmosphere wash over you.

As you prepare to create your own unforgettable memories in Copenhagen, I invite you to share your experiences with others. Whether through social media, travel blogs, or simply storytelling, sharing your journey can inspire others to explore this wonderful city and connect with its many facets. The beauty of travel lies not only in the places you visit but in the stories you gather along the way and the connections you make with people and places.

In closing, remember that every adventure in Copenhagen is an opportunity to see the world from a new perspective, to embrace the unfamiliar, and to create memories that will last a lifetime. The city's blend of history, culture, and natural beauty offers endless possibilities for discovery, and I hope that your journey through Copenhagen leaves you with a sense of wonder, a deeper appreciation for the world around you, and a collection of experiences that will stay with you long after you've returned home.

MAP
Scan QR Code with device to view map for easy navigation

Printed in Great Britain
by Amazon